Choices & Changes
IN LIFE, SCHOOL, AND WORK
Grades 2–4

Choices & Changes
IN LIFE, SCHOOL,
AND WORK
Grade 2–4

D1520044

NCEE

National Council on Economic Education

*This publication was made possible through funding of the
Calvin K. Kazanjian Economics Foundation.*

Author

Jim Charkins is professor of economics at California State University, San Bernardino and Executive Director of the California Council on Economic Education. Dr. Charkins served on the 10-member writing team for Kindergarten through Twelfth Grade national economics standards. He has worked with the California Department of Education to develop a Kindergarten through 12th grade economics curriculum. He served as the economics content consultant to the California Commission for the Establishment of Academic Content and Performance Standards. He has written many curricula for the National Council on Economic Education and has been a pioneer in the use of literature to help children learn economics. He has conducted economic education workshops for teachers across the nation from Kindergarten through graduate school.

ISBN 1-56183-580-3

5 4 3 2 1

Contents

Acknowledgments

The author and the National Council on Economic Education express their deepest gratitude to the many individuals who were involved with this project.

Reviewers:
Dawn Cushing, Teacher, Cucamonga Middle School, CA
Cindy Morris, Reading Specialist, Moreno Valley Unified School District, CA
Barbara Phipps, Director, Center for Economic Education, University of Kansas, Lawrence, KS
Mary Lynn Reiser, Associate Director, Center for Economic Education, University of Nebraska, Omaha, NE
Mary Jo Skillings, Professor, Language, Literature and Culture, California State University, San Bernardino, CA
Susan Verducci, Center on Adolescence, Stanford University, CA

Teachers involved in field testing:
Kari Ito, Noddin Elementary School, CA
Megan Senini, Noddin Elementary School, CA
Ailish Johnson, Noddin Elementary School, CA
Fran Filice, Noddin Elementary School, CA

Foreword

The purpose of *Choices and Changes* is to teach elementary students how our economic system works so that they may enhance their own lives. Students learn that life is not a lottery—that there are steps they can follow while they are in elementary school to improve their opportunities for future success.

As students learn about decision-making, they also learn about the need to take responsibility for their decisions. They find out that the decisions they make today lead to changes in their future lives. They must carefully consider the alternatives available when making decisions and frequently reevaluate their decisions.

Choices and Changes focuses on using resources—particularly human capital—wisely. Human capital analysis is one of the most powerful concepts in economics, and *Choices and Changes* brings this analysis down to the elementary school level. Students make choices based on costs and benefits, and these choices will affect the rest of their lives. Investing in education, good work habits, and a healthy lifestyle will not only improve their future earnings but also result in a more satisfying life.

Choices and Changes will work with your students because the materials emphasize active learning. Students will enjoy the *Choices and Changes* lessons because they involve popular children's literature and a variety of hands-on activities. For example, they have the opportunity to organize and present a service project in their school or community. "Homegrams" involve a "Homework Helper" with activities to be conducted at home.

The National Council on Economic Education is grateful to the Calvin K. Kazanjian Economics Foundation for providing the financial resources to underwrite this revision of Choices and Changes. We hope that teachers will use these materials to teach their students the steps to achieve successful lives as consumers, producers, citizens, and participants in the global economy.

Robert F. Duvall, Ph.D.
President & Chief Executive Officer
The National Council on Economic Education

Introduction

Dear Teacher,

Thanks so much for choosing *Choices and Changes*. The purpose of this series of lessons is to help children learn about their ability to make choices and their **responsibility** for the **consequences** of those choices. Decision-making is a skill that, like any other skill, is learned through practice. *Choices and Changes* introduces the six-step decision-making process and helps students practice this skill throughout the lessons.

A second purpose of *Choices and Changes* is to help students realize that they possess valuable **knowledge and skills** that economists call "human capital." The idea is to help students recognize that they are **powerful** individuals, and that the purpose of school is to further develop their human capital so that they can maximize the quantity and quality of their alternatives after school, giving them more control over their lives. Students learn that the choices they make concerning school have consequences now and in the future. They are introduced to the world of **work**, discovering that they are already workers, as they learn to read, write, perform mathematical analyses, and make choices among alternatives.

A third purpose is to help students understand an **economy** in terms of **consumption** and **production**. Students learn about resources and discover that their human capital can be combined with other resources to produce goods and services. They learn that markets allow producers and consumers to exchange goods and services. They also learn that this **interdependence** is "risky business" as consumers depend on producers to provide goods and services and producers depend upon consumers to buy their products. Finally, students visualize themselves as producers in an economy of the future.

The lessons are meant to be integrated across the curriculum, and they lend themselves to active learning. They can be used to teach language arts, fine arts, and social studies. While the emphasis is on economics, each lesson begins with a story and uses the story to help students learn the economics. Lessons are developed around one or two books, but other books are listed which could be used as well, depending upon your current library and the ethnic makeup of your students. *Choices and Changes* provides a pedagogy that can be used with different books and different children at different grade levels.

The **student journals** help children keep track of what they are learning and enable them to develop a perspective on the entire set of lessons. The lessons include many tools that are introduced in a specific lesson, but they can be used in many other lessons as well. These tools include a report card, a help wanted ad, a job application, a letter of recommendation, a human capital inventory, a "menu" that helps students identify resources used in any production activity, a decision-making apron, and an alternative tree. The tools can also be adapted to different grade levels. For example, a report card with letter grades might not be used in your school until the third grade. If this is the case and you are a first grade teacher, simply use the report that you use to evaluate student performance.

Service learning is an integral part of *Choices and Changes*. In unit one, children will consider a number of alternatives for service learning. In units two, three, and four they can carry out their projects. Various alternatives are suggested for service-learning projects. Many of the lessons will have service-learning objectives. Some lessons contain letters called "Homegrams." These letters can be sent to the student's homework helper. They are meant to keep the adults informed about *Choices and Changes* activities and to elicit adult involvement.

The books listed in this volume have been selected based on the following criteria. Can they be used to help students learn the lesson? Are they grade-appropriate? Are they colorful and entertaining? Can children of different ethnic groups identify with the characters? In general, you probably will not want to use more than two books per lesson. Each lesson suggests a large number of books so that you can choose appropriate titles from the books that are available to you.

The lessons can be approached in different ways. A school-wide curricular decision might place some lessons in kindergarten, some in grade 1, grade 2, etc., or a teacher acting individually might decide to teach the entire series of lessons. Some books are especially suitable for use at certain grade levels, although most of them may be used at more than one level. The teaching techniques can be modified for individual class characteristics.

Choices and Changes is not meant to be a series of lesson plans that must be followed step by step with no variation. Upon first use, you might benefit from following the recommended steps closely, taking advantage of the logic and sequencing plan the lessons provide. As you gain more experience with *Choices and Changes*, however, you will no doubt develop adaptations of your own to help your students meet the lesson objectives. Once you master the underlying approach in this way, *Choices and Changes* truly becomes your own. We hope you and your students will enjoy the process.

Economics is a subject that frightens many people. Especially to those who are strangers to it, it seems remote and difficult, and many would claim that it has no place in the K-12 curriculum. But the fundamental concepts in economics are not difficult and can be extremely helpful to students as they make decisions during the K-12 years. The basic concept in economics is *scarcity,* which implies that our resources are insufficient to satisfy all our wants; all else stems from this concept. Note that the concept of scarcity does not mean there are insufficient resources to feed or clothe the world; it says that resources are insufficient to satisfy all our *wants* (electronic equipment, gas guzzling cars, vacations, fast food, and much more). The concept of scarcity is not a moral one; it does not make judgments about people's wants, it simply states that resources are insufficient to satisfy all our wants. As a result, we make choices.

Economic choices involve allocating resources and goods and services among alternatives. Many students recognize that they have to make choices about spending their limited income. Some have allowances, some have jobs, some have gifts from adults, but most have had to decide at one time or another how to "allocate" or spend their limited income. One of the goals of *Choices and Changes* is to help students generalize from the concept of scarcity to understand that all people, including their parents or other adults, have to make choices about allocating their limited income. As a result, neither children nor adults can have everything they want.

Economic choices involve allocating resources among *production* alternatives. Should the U.S. economy use its scarce resources to produce more educational services or more environmental purity? If both, how much of both? Perhaps the most important decision students make daily is what to produce with their limited *human capital*, their skills and knowledge. Human capital and decisions about how to develop it and what to do with it are major themes of *Choices and Changes*. While students don't often think of themselves as workers, *Choices and Changes* emphasizes the fact that they are, indeed, workers, and that their job in school is to develop their human capital. When deciding how to approach their schoolwork, for example, students may choose between work and leisure. This decision is highlighted throughout the lessons.

Some economic terms are used—not merely to teach vocabulary but to help students learn how to handle tasks of economic reasoning. The goal is for students to "own" the vocabulary so that it becomes a natural part of their thinking process. Once the terms are introduced, lesson procedures suggest ways to develop students' understanding of them.

The book at hand is a teacher resource manual. Many of the sections in the manual are not meant for students. The Economic and Affective Content sections are meant to help you understand the concepts that are introduced in the lesson. The teaching procedures will guide you through the presentation of the concepts to the students.

We hope that you and your students enjoy *Choices and Changes* and that the lessons help your students learn to become responsible and powerful economic citizens.

Sincerely,
R. J. Charkins

Correlation of *Choices and Changes in Life, School and Work* Lesson with the National Standards for the English Language Arts*

Standards	Lessons																	
	1	2	3	4	5	6	7	8	9	10	11	12	13	14	15	16	17	18
Students:																		
Read a wide range of print and nonprints texts to build an understanding of texts, of themselves, and of the cultures of the United States and the world; to acquire new information; to respond to the needs and demands of society and the workplace; and for personal fulfillment. Among these texts are fiction and nonfiction, classic and contemporary works.	•	•	•	•	•		•	•	•	•	•	•	•	•	•	•	•	•
Read a wide range of literature from many periods in many genres to build an understanding of the many dimensions (e.g., philsophical, ethical, aesthetic) of human experience.		•	•	•	•	•	•						•	•		•	•	•
Apply a wide range of strategies to comprehend, interpret, evaluate, and appreciate texts. Students draw on their prior experience, their interactions with other readers and writers, their knowledge of word meaning and of other texts, their word identification strategies, and their understanding of textual features (e.g., sound-letter correspondence, sentence structure, context, graphics).	•		•	•	•	•		•	•		•							•
Adjust their use of spoken, written and visual language (e.g., conversations, style, vocabulary) to communicate effectively with a variety of audiences and for different purposes.	•	•			•				•	•			•		•		•	•
Employ a wide range of strategies as they write and use different writing process elements appropriately to communicate with different audiences for a variety of purposes.	•								•		•							
Apply knowledge of language structure, language conventions (e.g., spelling and punctuation), media techniques, figurative language, and genre to create, critique, and discuss print and nonprint texts.	•			•				•								•		

Standards

Lessons

Standards	1	2	3	4	5	6	7	8	9	10	11	12	13	14	15	16	17	18
Students:																		
Conduct research on issues and interest by generating ideas and questions, and by posing problems. They gather, evaluate, and synthesize data from a variety of sources (e.g., print and nonprint texts, artifacts, people) to communicate their discoveries in ways that suit their purpose and audience.	•																	
Use a variety of technological and informational resources (e.g., libraries, databases, computer networks, video) to gather and synthesize information and to create and communicate knowledge.		•					•		•			•		•	•			
Participate as knowledgeable, reflective, creative, and critical members of a variety of literacy communities.	•	•	•	•	•	•	•			•						•		
Use spoken, written and visual language to accomplish their own purposes (e.g., for learning, enjoyment, persuasion, and the exchange of information).	•	•		•					•					•	•	•	•	•

*Standards taken from *Standards for the English Language Arts*, International Reading Association (IRA) and the National Council of Teachers of English (NCTE), 1996.

Correlation of *Choices and Changes in Life, School and Work* Lessons With the National Standards for Economics

Economic Standards Lessons

	1	2	3	4	5	6	7	8	9	10	11	12	13	14	15	16	17	18
1. Scarcity	•	•	•	•	•	•					•	•	•	•	•			
2. Marginal costs/marginal benefits	•	•	•	•	•													
3. Allocation of goods and services																		
4. Role of incentives																		
5. Gain from trade																•	•	•
6. Specialization and trade																		
7. Markets–price and quantity determination																•	•	•
8. Role of price in market system																		
9. Role of competition																		
10. Role of economic institutions																		
11. Role of money																		
12. Role of interest rates																		
13. Role of resources in determining income							•	•	•	•								

Choices and Changes in Life, School, and Work, © National Council on Economic Education, New York, NY

Economic Standards Lessons

	1	2	3	4	5	6	7	8	9	10	11	12	13	14	15	16	17	18
14. Profit and the entrepreneur																•	•	•
15. Growth																		
16. Role of government																		
17. Using cost/benefit analysis to evaluate government programs																		
18. Macroeconomy-income/employment, prices																		
19. Unemployment and inflation																		
20. Monetary and fiscal policy																		

UNIT ONE
CHOICES

UNIT ONE
Overview: I Can Make Choices

Unit 1 introduces the students to the process of decision making. The unit develops a step-by-step approach to the process, culminating in the use of the process itself. Important economic concepts are scarcity, alternatives, advantages and disadvantages, choice, and opportunity cost. Students learn that they have the power to make choices and that they are responsible for the consequences of their choices.

Lesson 1. Scarcity

Students read *The Berenstain Bears Get the Gimmes* and find out, through a classroom example, that scarcity means people can't have everything they want.

Lesson 2. Alternatives

Students read *Way Out West Lives a Coyote Named Frank* and *Tight Times* and learn to discover alternatives to overcome obstacles. They make a mobile to illustrate Frank's alternatives.

Lesson 3. Alternatives Have Advantages and Disadvantages

Students read *Tops and Bottoms* and study different vegetables to identify advantages and disadvantages of alternatives.

Lesson 4. Choice

Students read *Helga's Dowry: A Troll Love Story* and *Ferdinand the Bull* to learn about choices and personal responsibility. They use choice cards and a choice can to keep track of their choices.

Lesson 5. Opportunity Cost

Students read *Big Squeak, Little Squeak, Uncle Jed's Barbershop* and *A Day's Work* to discover that every choice has an opportunity cost. They use artwork to identify the opportunity cost of their decision. This lesson can be used with a unit on immigration.

Lesson 6. Decision Making

Students read *The King, the Mice, and the Cheese, Brandi's Braids, No Plain Pets,* and *Chicken Sunday* and use a decision-making apron and choice cards to learn the five-step decision-making process. This lesson can be used with a multi-cultural unit.

Lesson 1
Scarcity
Why don't people give you everything you want?

Cognitive Objectives:

Students will

- Define *scarcity* as people's inability to have everything they want.
- Identify examples of scarcity in their lives.

Affective Objective:

Students will

- Accept scarcity as a fact of life.

It is a paradox that people who learn to accept and deal with scarcity often achieve much more than those who don't accept it. The inability to deal with scarcity leads to problems with money, education, skill development, and many other areas. If children accept scarcity, they can then develop the skills necessary to minimize its impact on their lives. They will realize, for example, that credit provides only a postponement of the results of scarcity, not its elimination. Acceptance of scarcity may also prompt people to discover alternatives that can minimize its effects.

Service-learning Objective:

Students will

- Identify examples of scarcity faced by individuals, their school, and their community, where the class might be able to help.

Required Book

- *The Berenstain Bears Get the Gimmes*

Optional Books

- *If You Give a Mouse a Cookie*
- *If You Give a Moose a Muffin*
- *If You Give a Pig a Pancake*

Required Materials

- Candy, nuts, fruit, small "favors" or other items that students are sure to want. There should be an insufficient number, so that not every child can receive an item.
- Student Journal, page 1-1
- Homegram 1

Economics Background for Teachers

Scarcity is the basic economic problem. It arises from the insufficiency of resources to satisfy people's wants.

Scarcity is ubiquitous. Rich people face scarcity when they want more than they can buy, when they can't be in two places at once, and when, accordingly, they must choose among alternatives. Some people take exception to the statement that rich people face scarcity, thinking that it implies sympathy for the rich. But scarcity is not a matter of sympathy; it is merely a fact about the relationship between unlimited wants and limited resources. As people's resources grow, their wants also grow. Poor people face scarcity, too, of course, but scarcity is not the same thing as poverty. Poverty can be defined as income below a certain level, but scarcity simply means that people's resources are insufficient to satisfy their wants. Selfish people face scarcity, but so do selfless people who want to help others.

Scarcity, therefore, is not a problem that can be solved, but it is a condition that people can address in a rational manner in order to improve their lives. How? By making choices. Since resources are scarce in relation to wants, people must decide how they will use those resources. This is so even for the most advantaged among us, since resources are finite. If they weren't—if scarcity didn't exist—people would never have to choose. But people encounter scarcity all the time, and they find, therefore, that they must respond by making choices.

Vocabulary

- **Scarcity:** The condition of not being able to have all of the goods and services one wants.

Getting Started

Explain that the class is beginning an important unit of study—one that can help students be more successful in accomplishing their goals today and in the future. Ask the students to repeat the name *Choices and Changes.* Tell them that they will learn more about that name over the next few weeks. During that time they will actually be studying a way to make choices. The name for this area of study is *economics.* Write the word "economics" on the board. The students should repeat the word and its definition as *the study of decision making.* Economics helps people make choices about work, learning, money, and many other activities. Using economics can help us become the kind of students and workers that we choose to be.

Distribute the *Student Journals* and explain that these journals are for the students to keep, not only during the unit but always. Completing work in the journals will be important to their success in *Choices and Changes,* since the journal entries will highlight new learning and suggest ways in which new learning may be applied, now and in the future. Give the students a chance to look through their journals.

Teaching Procedures

1. Have the students read (or read to them) *The Berenstain Bears Get the Gimmes.* In this story, the bear cubs see things they want everywhere—at the supermarket, the mall, on TV, and so on. Mama and Papa Bear finally put a limit on the cubs' unlimited wants.

2. Introduce the concept of *scarcity.* Tell the students that the concept means we can't have everything we want.

- Write the word "scarcity" on the board. Have students repeat the word.
- Discuss scarcity. Mama and Papa Bear couldn't give the cubs everything they wanted. Teachers can't give students everything they want, such as pencils, paper, and other school supplies, because these things are scarce. Parents can't give children everything they want, such as toys, trips to amusement parks, or special clothes, because these things are scarce. Scarcity is the reason we can't have or do everything we want. The bear cubs weren't willing to accept the fact of scarcity, so they cried and acted like babies. Once Mama and Papa Bear stepped in, the cubs began to act more properly. Accepting scarcity is the first

step toward learning what to do about it. That is what this class is about—learning to deal with scarcity.

3. Bring something to class that the students will want (such as candy, nuts, or other food or some small "favors"). Don't bring enough for every student.

- Explain that you would like to distribute the items to the class, but you can't do it unless everyone can have an item, and you are not allowed to split items.
- Put the items away and explain that the problem is scarcity. With the supply of items you have, there are not enough to satisfy everyone's wants. Explain that you know this is a disappointment, but scarcity often makes us disappointed. (Note: It is important at this point to maintain the condition of scarcity. Do not ask the students to suggest ways to solve the problem, since scarcity is not a problem that can be solved.)
- Emphasize that *because of scarcity* we can't have everything we want. The items you brought to class were scarce in comparison to the students' wants; there weren't enough items to satisfy the class.

4. Ask the students to identify real-life situations in which they have experienced scarcity. Ask them how they react when their parents tell them that they can't have something they want. Do they act like the bear cubs or do they understand that the problem is scarcity and accept it? How will they act in the future?

Service Learning

Tell the students that scarcity affects everyone. As a result, everyone could use some help with jobs he or she can't do alone. Tell the students that they will identify a project that will involve them in helping somebody cope with a scarcity situation. They should begin thinking about what that problem might be and what sort of help they might provide.

Assessment

Ask the students to open their journals to page 1-1. Have them brainstorm some examples of scarcity faced by individual people they know, or examples from their school or their community. Then ask them to list some of these examples in the space provided. (Note: You may want to screen these examples to make sure that no entries could be a source of embarrassment to anyone.)

Follow Through

To help the students recognize the pervasiveness of scarcity, point out examples of scarcity as they arise in the classroom and in the school. For example, if you have limited computers in the classroom and all the students would like to work on them, explain that scarcity doesn't allow everyone to work on the computers at the same time. Scarcity is the problem. Similar situations might occur with sports equipment, classroom supplies, and other areas.

Homegram

Distribute *Homegram 1* and ask the students to take it home and give it to their Homework Helper. If "Parent's Night" is early in the year, you may want to go over this with the parents at that time.

STUDENT JOURNAL Page 1-1

Some Examples of Scarcity
People Can't Have Everything They Want

1.

2.

3.

4.

HOMEGRAM
Lesson 1

Dear Homework Helper,

Over the next few weeks, the children and I will be involved in a unit of study called *Choices and Changes.* It is an economics unit and children will be learning about choices and the changes that result from those choices. The children are likely to be asking you about some of the choices that you have made. It will be very helpful if you will spend some time with your student helping him or her learn what choices are, the changes that choices can make, and the importance of thinking about decisions.

In the first unit of the program, the children will learn that they can't have everything they want, a situation economists call scarcity. They will learn to deal with scarcity, trying to find alternatives. Next, they will discover that every alternative has advantages and disadvantages and that they should think about the advantages and disadvantages of their alternatives before making decisions. They will learn to use a five-step decision-making process to help make decisions. Finally, they will learn that every choice has an opportunity cost.

One aspect of the lessons is reading. Each lesson uses one or two books to help students learn the ideas. If you would like the titles of the books so that you can purchase them or get them from the library and read them or have your student read them at home, I will be happy to give you a list. Reading with your student is a very effective way of helping him or her learn to read.

There are two very important outcomes of this unit. First, children learn that they have the power to make decisions. The more you can allow them to make decisions at home, the more effective this unit will be. We will be telling them that their attitude is a decision, their willingness to cooperate at school and at home is a decision, and their remembering to bring their homework to school is a decision.

The second important outcome is that children take responsibility for their decisions. At school, we will be holding them accountable for their decisions. The lessons of *Choices and Changes* will be applied in our classroom. Children will learn that the teacher is not the "bad guy" but that they (the children) control their lives and cause consequences by making choices. The child is responsible for the choices and the consequences. I encourage you to help your student recognize decisions that he or she makes at home and to accept responsibility for the consequences of those decisions.

Sincerely,

Lesson 2
Alternatives

Is there anything else we can do?

Cognitive Objectives:

Students will

- Define *alternatives* as opportunities from which people choose.
- Identify alternatives that others face.
- Identify alternatives that they face.
- Identify alternatives to overcome obstacles.
- Make a mobile that represents two "alternative trees."

Affective Objectives:

Students will

- Look for alternatives instead of thinking they have "no choice."
- Address obstacles in a positive way.

In working on *Choices and Changes*, students should learn that they can ordinarily respond to events in their lives by alternative means, and that it is up to them in these cases to find an alternative that will result in a beneficial outcome. In Lesson 2, students begin to develop the skill of discovering alternatives. The point to be grasped is that people who find alternatives are more active and powerful than those who merely "let things happen to them." The more alternatives that can be discovered in a given case, the greater the students' ability to deal with scarcity.

Service Learning Objectives:

Students will

- List groups or individuals in the school or community whom they could help.
- List actions they might take to help each individual or group.
- Combine the two lists in an alternative tree.

Required Books

- *Way Out West Lives a Coyote Named Frank*
- *Tight Times*
- *The Rag Coat*

Optional Books

- *Something from Nothing*
- *If You Made a Million*
- *Amigo*

Required Materials

- Overhead transparency of Activity 2–1
- Overhead transparency of Service-Learning Project Alternative Tree
- Overhead transparency of Visual 2-1
- Obstacle Cards
- *Student Journal,* pages 2-1, 2-2, 2-3, and 2-4
- *Homegram 2*

Optional Materials

- Wire coat hangers and other materials to use in making a mobile
- Art supplies for the mobile

Economics Background for Teachers

Because of scarcity, people must choose among alternatives. The greater the number of alternatives identified, the more likely it is that the outcome will be beneficial. People often fail to identify all the alternatives available to them, which means that they miss opportunities. When people face obstacles, they often make the statement, "I had no choice." What they really mean is that they had too few alternatives or the alternatives they faced were not very attractive.

In attempting to reach goals, people often face obstacles. To deal successfully with the obstacles, people must find alternative ways to do what they want to do. When they can find more and better alternatives, they improve their chance of achieving their goals.

Vocabulary

- **Alternatives:** Opportunities (possible things or actions) from which people choose.
- **Goal:** Something that a person wants to have or do.
- **Obstacle:** Something that gets in people's way as they seek to reach a goal.

Getting Started

Tell the students that they are going to find different ways of doing things today. They are going to begin to identify *alternatives*. Alternatives are opportunities (possible things or actions) from which people choose.

Teaching Procedures

1. Have the students read *Way Out West Lives a Coyote Named Frank*. Frank is a coyote who has two friends, Larry and Melanie. Regarding friends to play with and things to do, Frank has many alternatives. He can play with Larry or Melanie or he can be by himself. When he plays with Larry, they usually chase rabbits or dig up homes of mice. When he plays with Melanie, they usually bother burros or other animals. When he is by himself, Frank often reads, starts new hobbies, or just sleeps. At night he gets together with the other coyotes to howl at the moon.

2. Have the students turn to page 2-1 in their journals and complete the "Alternatives Tree" for Frank. They can complete the boxes by writing or drawing. (Answers are provided at the end of this lesson.) Explain that Frank has alternatives as to which friends he will play with, and he has more alternatives as to what he might do with the different friends. The tree activity helps children identify these alternatives. Have the students repeat the word "alternative" and review the point that alternatives are opportunities (things or actions) from which people choose. Have the students make a mobile to represent Frank's alternatives, based on their work on the decision tree. Hang the mobiles in the classroom.

3. Read the story *Tight Times*. Before beginning the story, tell the children that you are going to ask them to identify some of the alternatives the young narrator and his family face. Display an overhead transparency of Activity 2-1. In the book, a young boy wants a dog, but his parents tell him he can't have one because of

"tight times." Because of tight times the family eats bulk cereal instead of cereal in little boxes; they run through the sprinkler instead of going to the lake; they have soup with lima beans instead of roast beef for Sunday dinner; they hire a child-care provider so Mom can work outside the home; and the boy gets a cat (whom he names Dog) instead of a dog. After reading the story, ask the children to complete Activity 2-1. In this activity they identify alternatives for cereal, water play, Sunday dinner, child care, and a pet. Emphasize that the boy and his family had to choose from alternatives. Because of tight times, the problem of scarcity was even more difficult, and the boy and his family had to find the best possible alternative.

4. Introduce the concepts of *goals* and *obstacles*. Explain to the class that goals are things that people want to have or do, and obstacles are things that get in people's way as they seek to reach their goals. Write the words "goal" and "obstacle" on the board. Explain that an important skill is finding alternative ways to overcome obstacles and reach a goal.

5. Read the story *The Rag Coat*. Repeat the point that a goal is something a person wants to have or do. Ask the following questions.

- What is Minna's goal? (*Minna wants to go to school.*)
- What obstacle does she face? (*She doesn't have a coat.*)
- What alternative did Mrs. Miller suggest to overcome the obstacle? (*The ladies could make a coat from scraps.*)
- Minna wanted to go to school, but she faced another obstacle when she wore her coat to school. What was that obstacle? (*The other children at school laughed at her coat, calling it a bunch of rags.*)
- Minna could have gone home or she could have returned to school. Which alternative did she choose? (*She returned to school.*)
- How did she overcome the obstacle of the other children making fun of her? (*She told the stories that each patch in her coat represented.*)

6. Have the students form teams of two. Distribute eight of the obstacle cards so that each team has one card. There may be duplicates, which means that teams who have the same cards should work together. (You will use the other six obstacle cards in Lesson 3.) Have members from each team explain their obstacle and some alternative ways to deal with the obstacle. In discussing the alternatives, explain why dealing with obstacles is much better than trying to ignore them.

7. Make a list of the suggested alternatives, but do not make any evaluative comments about good or bad aspects of them. Collect the obstacle cards.

Service Learning

You may want to wait until Unit 4 to decide on the service-learning project. In the meanwhile, however, students should look at some possible projects so that they can be thinking about the service-learning project as they progress through *Choices and Changes*. Toward this end, remind the students that all of them will do a service-learning project. Explain that *service learning* means learning by doing something for someone else—that is, by providing a service. Explain that they will begin considering some alternatives for the service-learning project. Present the list of alternatives shown in the *Student Journals* on page 2-2, and tell the students that they are welcome to add to the list at any time. They also should talk service-learning possibilities over with adults at home and elsewhere to see if they can broaden the range of alternative possibilities.

When you do begin to choose a project, have the students review their lists of alternatives as they work to identify groups or individuals for whom they could provide a service. Some alternatives might involve friends or relatives, the school, the community, the aged, or the homeless. After discussion, help the students narrow the range to three or four alternatives. Then move to a consideration of what actions the class might take to help the individuals or groups in question. There are really two questions: for whom do you want to provide a good or service and what do you want to do for them? You can begin with either. For example, the class might decide first that they want to do something for the homeless and decide next what it is that they might do. Or the class might decide first to make a quilt and then decide for whom to make it.

Have the students turn to page 2-3 in their journals and complete an alternative tree for their service-learning project. (There is a blank alternative tree at the end of this lesson. You can make a transparency of the tree and work through it with the students.)

Assessment

Sometimes alternatives are good ones and sometimes they are not. Have the students turn to page 2-4 in their journals and circle the alternatives they would select. At this point, it is not necessary to have them explain their selections; the idea is simply to help them identify alternatives.

Follow Through

Be on the lookout for new opportunities to engage students in thinking about alternatives. When students make excuses for not having completed a task, for example, ask whether they had investigated alternative courses of action that might have helped to avoid or otherwise deal with the obstacle that kept them from completing that task.

Getting Ready for Tomorrow

Ask the students to bring in a clean, empty can from home. The can should be covered with aluminum foil and free of sharp points. The children won't use the can until Lesson 4, but this will give them a couple of days to bring them in.

Homegram

Distribute *Homegram 2* and ask the children to take it home and give it to their Homework Helper.

STUDENT JOURNAL Page 2-1

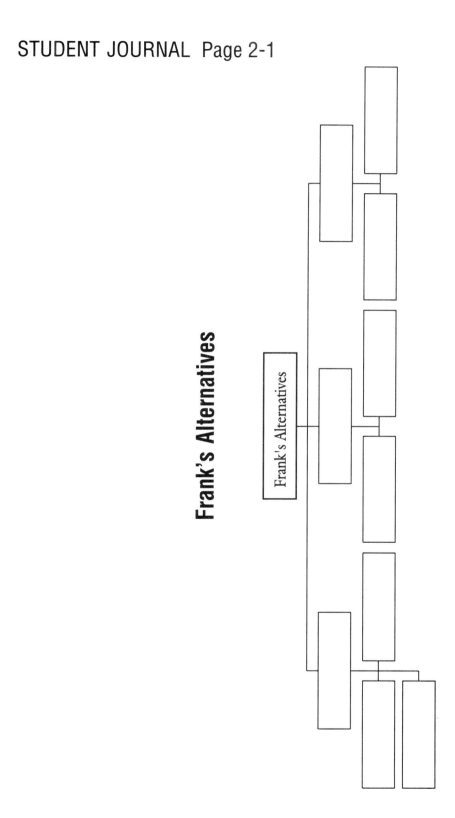

Frank's Alternatives

STUDENT JOURNAL Page 2-2
Service-Learning Alternative

Lesson 3: Plant a school garden.

Lesson 5: Develop respect for others by creating a cultural awareness program through reading, food, art, and clothing. Make one day each month a cultural awareness day.

Lesson 14: Bake some goods at home and bring them to a homeless shelter, a food pantry, or some other area of need.

Lesson 15: Perform the play *Treemonisha* for a younger class or a group of senior citizens.

Make a quilt for . . . .

During the holidays, buy and deliver a holiday meal basket containing ham, turkey, roast beef, or another main course, plus canned vegetables and other non-perishable food.

Develop a school pride clean-up day, doing whatever work is necessary to improve the appearance of the school.

Host an appreciation day for non-teaching staff at the school.

Read to seniors or kindergartners in the community.

Beautify the school grounds.

Interview an elderly immigrant couple about their journey to America and their experiences since they arrived. Draw pictures or collect photos and make a quilt for them.

STUDENT JOURNAL Page 2-3

An Alternative Tree for the Service-Learning Project

The Alternative Tree

STUDENT JOURNAL Page 2-4
Alternatives I Would Select

Circle the alternative you would select.

1. The school cafeteria is offering hot dogs or veggie burgers. Which alternative do you select?

   Hot Dog   Veggie Burger

2. Your teacher has asked you to read a book out loud to the class. Your alternatives are *Way Out West Lives a Coyote Named Frank* or *Tight Times*. Which alternative do you select?

   Frank   *Tight Times*

3. You can't decide whether to read or play with a friend after school. Which alternative do you select?

   Read   Play

4. It is 8:00 at night and you are pretty tired. You would like to get some sleep and you also would like to see a special TV show. Which alternative do you select?

   TV   Sleep

5. You are out to dinner and have to decide on dessert. Your alternatives are ice cream or fruit pie. Which alternative do you select?

   Ice Cream   Fruit Pie

Activity 2-1
The Search for Alternatives

Identify two alternatives for cereal, water play,
Sunday dinner, child care, and a pet.

Cereal   _____   _____

Water play   _____   _____

Sunday dinner   _____   _____

Child care   _____   _____

Pet   _____   _____

VISUAL 2-1

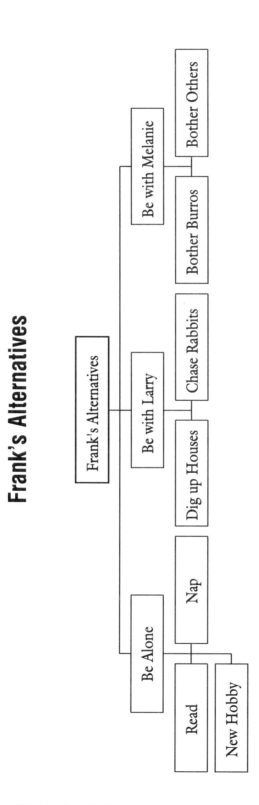

Frank's Alternatives

Frank's Alternatives

Be with Larry
Chase Rabbits
Dig up Houses

Be with Melanie
Bother Others
Bother Burros

Be Alone
Nap
Read
New Hobby

Obstacle Cards

You want to read a certain book, but you don't have the money to buy it.	You want a good grade on an assignment, but it is due tomorrow and your favorite TV show is on tonight.
You and your best friend have an argument and you want to make up, but he or she won't listen to you.	You want to go to the movies next Saturday, but you don't have the money.
You decide that you want to learn to read very well, but you aren't making much progress.	You want to get home to help your mom with dinner, but a lot of kids are going to the mall to hang out. You want to go with them.
A kid offers you drugs on the playground. You don't want to take them, but you are afraid not to.	You are hungry and want to eat lunch, but you spent your lunch money on candy.

Choices and Changes in Life, School, and Work, © National Council on Economic Education, New York, NY

Obstacle Cards (continued)

You agree to play with a friend on Saturday, but then someone you like better asks you to play. You don't want to be mean to either of your friends.	Your parents want you to visit your aunt on the weekend, but a friend has asked you to go to the zoo.
You forgot to bring a can for a *Choices and Changes* project. The other kids all have them. You wish you had remembered.	You want to tell your friend something very important, but you will get in trouble if you talk to her in class.
You want to save money for gifts for the holidays, but you don't get an allowance and you don't have much money.	Your class is doing a play for the parents on Thursday night. You are supposed to be there, but you don't have a ride.

HOMEGRAM
Lesson 2

Dear Homework Helper,

In a few days, your student will be keeping track of the choices that he or she makes. I will give them blank choice cards that they are to complete and place in their "choice cans."

Would you please help your student make the can and remind him or her to bring it to school? It should be an empty, clean can with no rough edges, covered with aluminum foil.

Thank you so much for your help.

Sincerely,

Lesson 3
Alternatives Have Advantages and Disadvantages
What consequences do choices have?

Cognitive Objectives:

Students will

- Define *consequence* as something that happens as a result of an action or event.
- Define *advantage* as a desirable (good) consequence of an alternative.
- Define *disadvantage* as an undesirable (bad) outcome of an alternative.
- Identify advantages and disadvantages of alternatives.

Affective Objectives:

Students will

- Realize that alternatives have advantages and disadvantages.
- Accept responsibility for advantages and disadvantages of alternatives selected.
- Identify the advantages and disadvantages of alternatives before making choices.

Service-Learning Objective:

Students will

- Narrow the list of service-learning alternatives to two and map out a list of advantages and disadvantages of both alternatives.

Required Book

- *Tops and Bottoms*

Optional Books

- *The Three Little Pigs and the Fox*
- *Fifty-five Grandmas and a Llama*
- *Finders Keepers—Franklin*
- *Wolf's Stew*
- *The Great Migration*

Required Materials

- Any vegetable with tops and bottoms such as:
  Corn with the silk on it
  A head of lettuce
  A carrot with a top
  A radish
  A turnip
- List of alternatives for the service-learning project
- A decision-making apron (see instructions below)
- Paper and crayons or pencil for writing or drawing
- *Student Journals*, pages **3-1, 3-2, 3-3, 3-4**

Economics Background for Teachers

People often think that economics is about money. In *Choices and Changes*, students will discover that economics is about choosing among alternatives. Every alternative comes with advantages and disadvantages, and the most important of these often have nothing to do with money. When people lie, they lose the trust of others. That loss is a serious disadvantage, and we can use economic analysis to understand it. When a teacher does a good job with a lesson, the advantage may be a well-earned sense of achievement and pride arising from the initial choice to work hard in preparing the lesson. When a child learns to ride a bicycle, she or he may incur some risk of involvement in a bicycle-related mishap, but along with that risk she or he will gain a potential advantage of increased mobility. Both the disadvantage of increased risk and the advantage of increased mobility can be understood through economic analysis, even though no money is involved in either case.

Vocabulary

- **Advantage:** A desirable consequence of an alternative.
- **Consequence:** Something that happens as a result of an action or event.
- **Disadvantage:** An undesirable consequence of an alternative.

Getting Started

Remind the students that they have already begun to learn about alternatives in a prior lesson. They were able to identify alternatives in their reading about Frank, the coyote, and Minna, the girl in *The Rag Coat*. They learned that finding alternatives is a way to overcome obstacles. Emphasize that every alternative may have good and bad points. Tell them that they will learn more today about identifying the advantages and disadvantages of various alternatives.

Teaching Procedures

1. Tell the students that advantages are the good aspects of an alternative and disadvantages are the negative or bad aspects of an alternative. Write the words "advantages" and "disadvantages" on the board. (If you like, you can make a happy face next to "advantages" and a sad face next to "disadvantages.") Today the students will investigate the advantages and disadvantages of alternatives.

2. Read *Tops and Bottoms* to the class. Bear owns a great deal of land, but he is very lazy. Hare is poor and has lots of mouths to feed. Hare suggests a partnership to Bear, and Bear agrees, but he doesn't investigate the consequences of the alternatives he selects. Explain to the class that Bear chose three different alternatives and failed to consider their disadvantages. Continue the discussion as follows:

- When Bear chose the tops, what alternative did Hare select? Show the students one of the plants that Hare planted. (*He chose to plant carrots, radishes, and beets. For these plants, only the bottoms are good to eat.*)
- When Bear chose bottoms, what alternative did Hare select? Show the students one of the plants that Hare planted. (*He chose to plant lettuce, broccoli, and celery. For these plants, only the tops are good to eat.*)
- When Bear chose both tops and bottoms, what alternative did Hare select? Show the students some corn. (*He planted corn, where the tops [the tassels] and the bottoms [the stalks] are not good; only the middles are good to eat.*)
- What was the disadvantage of the tops alternative for Bear? (*The tops of carrots, radishes, and beets are not good to eat.*)
- What was the disadvantage of the bottoms alternative for Bear? (*The bottoms of lettuce, broccoli, and celery are not good to eat.*)
- What was the disadvantage of the tops and bottoms alternative for Bear? (*The tops [silk] and the bottoms [stalks] are not good to eat.*)
- Instead of just saying "tops" or "bottoms," what alternatives might Bear have proposed to Hare? (*He could have asked Hare what he was going to plant; he could have suggested that they split the crop; he could have planted his fields himself.*)

- Did Bear think about his alternatives? *(No.)*
- What advantages did Hare gain from the alternatives Bear chose? *(Hare could choose to plant anything he wanted so that he always got the good part of the plant.)*
- Do you think Hare treated Bear properly? Would you trust Hare? *(Answers will vary.)*
- Have the class investigate two alternatives for Bear:
  ➤ 1. He could sleep and let Hare decide what to plant, or
  ➤ 2. He could pay attention and decide with Hare what crops to plant.

  If Bear chose alternative 2, he and Hare would have to find alternative ways to share the crops. Have the students identify the advantages and disadvantages of alternatives 1 and 2 for Bear.

3. Procedure 4 will involve use of a decision-making apron. The apron has eight pockets. The bottom pocket is labeled "GOAL" and is located at the bottom in the middle of the apron. Above the goal pocket are two more to either side; each of these pockets is labeled "ALTERNATIVES." Above each of the ALTERNATIVES pockets should be two pockets labeled (on each side) "DISADVANTAGES" and "ADVANTAGES." (You may wish to put a sad face on the DISADVANTAGES pockets and a happy face on the ADVANTAGES pockets.) At the top of the apron should be a pocket labeled "CHOICE." The pockets should be large enough to put 3″ × 5″ cards inside. (For detailed instructions on making the apron, see instructions at the end of this lesson. An alternative is to make an apron from poster board and place it on a bulletin board.) Once you put the apron on (or move to the poster board apron), students will catch on to the fact that they are going to make a decision. In this lesson, however, they are simply going to identify the advantages and disadvantages of two of Bear's alternatives.

4. Distribute two index cards or pieces of paper to each student. Ask the students to use the cards or pieces of paper to draw a picture of Bear's two alternatives. When the students finish doing this, collect the drawings, discuss them, and put them in the pockets marked "ALTERNATIVES." Distribute more paper and ask the students to draw pictures of the advantages of alternative 1. Collect these drawings, too; then discuss them and put them in the pocket marked "ADVANTAGES" above the first ALTERNATIVES pocket. Repeat the procedure for the disadvantages of the first alternative, advantages of the second alternative, and disadvantages of the second alternative. Thank the students for all of their hard work.

5. Distribute the *Student Journals* and have the students turn to the decision-making apron on page 3-1. Point out that on this page the students will see two

alternatives to one of the obstacles they faced in Lesson 2. Work through the page with the students. As they identify one advantage and one disadvantage of each alternative, have them write their answers in the boxes provided. Allow them to abbreviate their answers. Sample answers are shown on page 36.

6. Direct the students' attention to page 3-2 in the journals. Ask the students to identify the advantages and disadvantages of the alternatives suggested.

7. Ask the students to evaluate the choices made by Bear and Hare, using a report card. They may use the report card shown in Activity 3-1, or one that is more suitable for your school and grade level. Project a transparency of the report card on the overhead. Discuss the report card with the students, explaining what each category means. Pair the children in teams of two. Have one of the children in each team complete a report card for Bear and have the other complete the card for Hare. They should then compare notes and see if they agree on the cards. Then select a few Bears and a few Hares and have them present their report cards to the class.

Service Learning

Remind the students of the alternatives that they discussed for their service-learning project. Write the alternatives on the board. Use a voting procedure to have the students narrow the range of alternatives to two. Erase the alternatives that were not chosen in this balloting. Then put on the decision-making apron and ask the students to provide ideas about the advantages and disadvantages of both alternatives. Write all of these on the board and have the students record them in their journals on page 3-3. (Since the students may actually do the project that gets selected, be sure that they view the advantages and disadvantages of each alternative realistically.)

Assessment

Divide the students into six small groups. Assign each of the groups one of the remaining (not yet discussed) Obstacle Cards from Lesson 2 and tell them that their task is to think of consequences for each of the alternatives printed on the cards. Explain that they will report back to the class when they are finished. They might approach the task by having one student read an alternative, another state possible advantages, and a third state possible disadvantages. Give the class about 10 minutes for work in their groups. Have them complete the table "Alternatives, Advantages, Disadvantages" (from page 3-3 in the *Student Journal*) for their goal and obstacle.

STUDENT JOURNAL Page 3-1

Decision-Making Apron

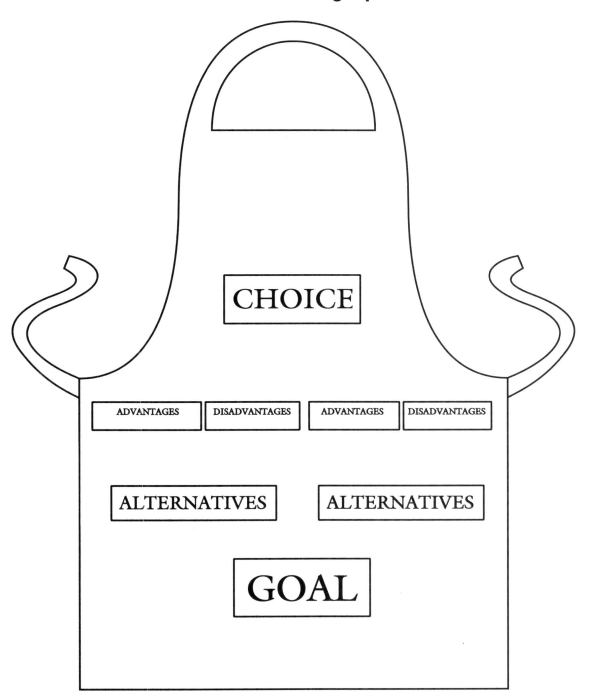

STUDENT JOURNAL Page 3-2
Obstacles and Alternatives

I want to read a certain book, but I don't have the money to buy it.

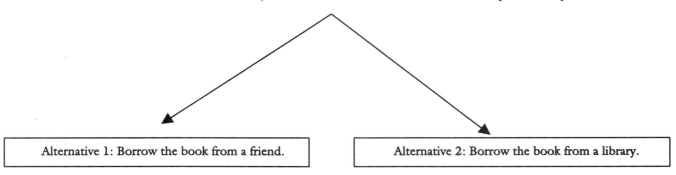

| Alternative 1: Borrow the book from a friend. | Alternative 2: Borrow the book from a library. |

I want a good grade, but my favorite TV show is on.

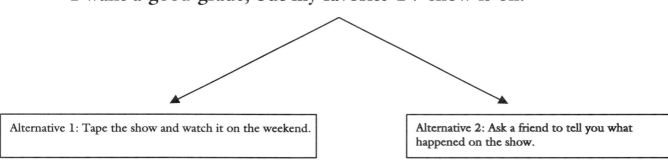

| Alternative 1: Tape the show and watch it on the weekend. | Alternative 2: Ask a friend to tell you what happened on the show. |

STUDENT JOURNAL Page 3-3

Alternatives, Advantages, and Disadvantages

Our Goal _____

Our Obstacle _____

Alternative 1		Alternative 2	
Advantages	Disadvantages	Advantages	Disadvantages

Our Goal _____

Our Obstacle _____

Alternative 1		Alternative 2	
Advantages	Disadvantages	Advantages	Disadvantages

Our Goal _____

Our Obstacle _____

Alternative 1		Alternative 2	
Advantages	Disadvantages	Advantages	Disadvantages

STUDENT JOURNAL Page 3-4

Our Service-Learning Project

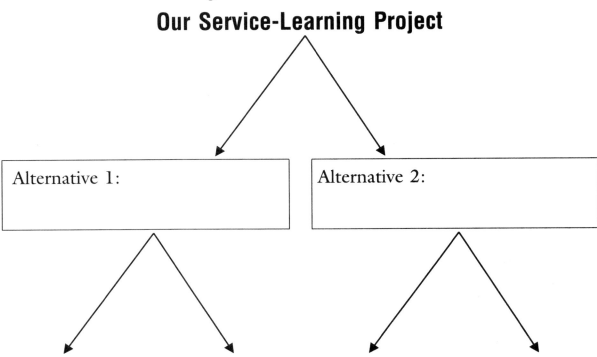

Advantages	Disadvantages	Advantages	Disadvantages

Activity 3-1
Report Card

A = OUTSTANDING
B = GOOD
C = SATISFACTORY
D = IMPROVEMENT NEEDED
F = FAILURE

NAME: _____

GRADE: _____

TEACHER: _____

WORK HABITS & ATTITUDES	GRADE	COMMENTS
1. USES TIME WISELY		
2. PAYS ATTENTION		
3. USES RESOURCES WISELY		
4. SETS GOALS		
5. DEVELOPS PLAN		
6. WORKS INDEPENDENTLY		
7. IS SELF-DIRECTED		
8. COMPLETES WORK		
9. IS RESPONSIBLE FOR MATERIALS		
10. IS HONEST AND FAIR		

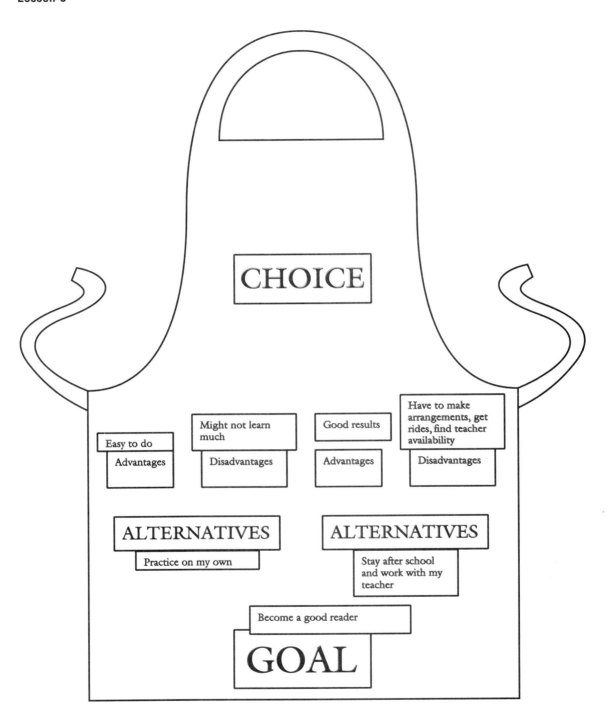

How to Make an Apron

1. Cut a square of fabric 20×20 inches. Finish the edges.

2. Cut another square of fabric 10×10 inches. Finish the edges.

3. Attach the smaller square to one side of the larger square. Make certain that it is centered. This will be the bib of the apron.

4. Use ribbon to make a tie for the waist (attached to the top of the larger square), and a tie for the neck (attached to the top of the smaller square).

5. Stitch pockets to accommodate decision-making cards. They should be arranged in the following order (on the bib of the apron):

CHOICE

Advantages   Disadvantages   Advantages   Disadvantages

Alternatives   Alternatives

GOAL

Lesson 4
Choice

How do the choices I make today affect the rest of my life?

Cognitive Objectives:

Students will

- Define *choice* as a selection from alternatives.
- Identify choices that they make.

Affective Objectives:

Students will

- Recognize that they have the power to make choices.
- Accept responsibility for the advantages and disadvantages of their choices.

In this lesson, students should recognize that they have the power to choose and that they do make many choices. Many people feel powerless because they think they don't make choices.

The purpose of this lesson is not to label particular choices as good or bad, but to identify choices and help students feel the power that comes with making choices. Students should recognize that they control their lives by the choices they make. Of course, it is true that parents and other people constrain the alternatives available to children. Nevertheless, children make choices day in and day out—concerning, for example, their attitudes in school and outside school, the amount of effort they put into their school work, and many other important and less important issues. They should know that an attitude involves a choice, and that the attitudes they choose to adopt have important effects on themselves and others. In addition, students should understand from this lesson that choice is a two-edged sword: they have the power to make choices and to enjoy the advantages those choices might bring; but they are also responsible for the disadvantages that may follow from their choices.

Required Books

- *Helga's Dowry: A Troll Love Story*
- *Ferdinand the Bull*

Optional Books

- *Three Billy Goats Gruff*
- *The Three Little Pigs and the Fox*
- *Jubal's Wish*
- *The Yellow Star*
- *The Snow Wife*
- *A Chair for My Mother*
- *Angelina and the Princess*
- *Alexander, Who's Not (Do you hear me? I mean it!) Going to Move*

Required Materials

- *Student Journal*, page 4-1
- Choice Cards: Enough for every student to have five (5)
- Art materials for children to use in making pictures
- Cans covered with aluminum foil
- Homegram 4
- Homework Helper's Choices

Economics Background for Teachers

The economics in this lesson is simple and straightforward. Students learn that choices are selections from alternatives. The main economics lesson is that we all make choices.

Vocabulary

- **Choice:** A selection from two or more alternatives.
- **Responsibility:** Accepting the consequences of choices.

Getting Started

Explain to the students that today's lesson is about choices. Write the word "choice" on the board and explain that a choice is a selection from **alternatives**.

Teaching Procedures

1. Tell the students that you are going to read them a story and you want them to find the choices that the main character, Helga, makes. Read *Helga's Dowry*. The book is about a beautiful troll named Helga who wants to marry Lars, a very handsome troll. But Helga has no dowry, so, unbeknown to Helga, Lars begins courting Inge, a fairly plain troll with a large dowry. Helga makes a journey to earn a dowry, and along the way she makes several decisions. When you come to a decision that Helga faces, stop and give the students a chance to identify her alternatives, her choice, and her reasons for choosing as she did. The discussion should focus on goals, obstacles, alternatives, advantages, and disadvantages. (Four of Helga's major choices were to take charge and go out and earn the dowry instead of sitting around and moping, to select from among alternative ways to earn the money, not to marry Lars, and to marry the king.) After you have finished reading the story, ask the following questions.

- At the beginning of the story, what was Helga's goal? *(Helga wanted to marry Lars.)* What obstacle did she face? *(She didn't have a dowry.)*
- What alternative means did Helga have for dealing with her obstacle? *(She could give up or she could earn the dowry.)*
- Did Helga's goals change as she worked to earn money? *(Yes. Initially the money was meant for Helga's dowry to marry Lars. But Helga figured out that Lars was not the only fish in the stream and, even if he were, Helga would be better off unmarried than married to egotistical and selfish Lars. Toward the end of the story, Helga chose to earn money for herself, not for Lars.)*
- How did Helga change? *(She became far more confident and independent. She chose to become a "liberated" woman.)*

2. Have the students complete a report card on Helga. *(Activity 3-1)*

3. Read *Ferdinand the Bull*. Ferdinand loves nothing better than sitting under a cork tree and smelling the flowers. When people from Madrid come to find bulls to fight in the ring, Ferdinand is smelling the flowers, but then a bee stings him. Ferdinand carries on something fierce, and the men from Madrid think he is very fierce. But in the bull ring Ferdinand returns to his true nature and refuses to fight. After you have finished reading the story, ask the following questions.

- What choice does Ferdinand make at the end of the story? *(Ferdinand goes against the "typical" path of bulls and chooses his preferred activity, sitting under the shade tree and smelling flowers.)*
- Ask the students whether they think Ferdinand made a good decision and why. What were his alternatives and what were the advantages and disadvantages of those alternatives? *(Answers will vary.)* NOTE: The same process can be used with the *Three Billy Goats Gruff* and *Three Little Pigs and the Fox*.

4. Explain to the students that they also make choices, just as Helga and Ferdinand did. Have the students do an art project, drawing a picture of their favorite character in either of the books. They may choose the character and the medium (crayons, paint, or other). Have them draw a picture of one of the character's choices. When they have completed their artwork, explain that they made many choices during the project. Ask them to identify those choices. Tell them that making a choice is a powerful action; the fact that they make choices makes them powerful people.

5. Have the students turn to page 4-1 of their journals. Have them look at the alternative characters they could have drawn and identify their choice by circling it. Ask them to explain why they chose the character they did.

6. Discuss other choices the students sometimes make: in choosing what clothes to wear, what to eat, what to do after school, whether to pay attention in school or not, how hard to try to learn, how to treat their friends and people they don't think of as friends, how brave to act when they are afraid, and so on.

- These choices have consequences. For example, students who choose to practice multiplication tables for 10 minutes or more will find their ability to do math problems will improve. If they decide not to work to get better at their multiplication tables, they may not be able to do future math problems that depend on multiplication skills; then their abilities in math will not improve. Our choices cause changes or consequences, both good and bad. This program of study is called *Choices and Changes* because it engages students in thinking about the choices they make and the changes (advantages and disadvantages) that their choices bring about.

- At this point, discuss the class rules. Tell the students that they choose to obey or disobey the rules. Explain that the word "responsibility" means accepting the consequences of choices. Write the word "responsibility" on the board. Develop a system of rewards and penalties for each rule. For example, at the end of each day, students who have chosen to obey all of the class rules get some "class money" that can be used at the end of the week or month to buy products in an auction. Every decision to break a rule can cost the students some of the "class money." Other disadvantages also may follow from disobeying class rules. For example, students who choose not to bring completed homework to class can stay in during recess to do the homework. (If the problem was the result of circumstances clearly outside of a student's control, then communication with the student's adult is important. The adults also must recognize the importance of children accepting the consequences of their choices. The concept of choices and consequences should be used in parent conferences so that parents understand that the students are being held responsible for the consequences of their choices.)

---

7. Tell the students that for the next five days they are going to keep track of the choices they make. Ask them to show you their aluminum cans. Tell them that these are their Choice Cans. The students will use the Choice Cans to keep track of the choices they make. At the end of the day for the next five days, distribute blank "A Choice I Made" cards and ask the students to use these cards to record their choices during the last 24 hours. They should put the cards in their Choice Cans, which should stay on top of their desks. During the first two days, remind them of some possible decisions that they might face such as what food to eat, clothing to wear, homework to do, TV to watch, and attitude to adopt in the classroom and on the playground.

Assessment

At the end of the five days, discuss with the students their most important choices, the advantages and disadvantages of those choices, and some alternatives that they might have chosen if their choices did not work out so well.

Follow Through

From now on, when the students select choices that have consequences for themselves and others, emphasize that they made the decision and accordingly they are responsible for both the advantages and the disadvantages of their choice.

Homegram

Send *Homegram 4* home with the students along with the page entitled "My Homework Helper's Choices." Have each student teach the Homework Helper what a choice is. Ask him or her to explain some choice that he or she has made in the last few days. Ask the students to fill out the page labeled "My Homework Helper's Choices" and bring it in the following day.

STUDENT JOURNAL Page 4-1
My Alternatives

Helga

Handsome Lars

Plain Inga

Old Sven   The King

Ferdinand

The Matador

Ferdinand's Mother

A Picadore

A Banderillero

The Bee

Choice Cards

"A Choice I Made"	"A Choice I Made"
I chose to _____	I chose to _____
One alternative I did not select was _____	One alternative I did not select was _____
"A Choice I Made"	"A Choice I Made"
I chose to _____	I chose to _____
One alternative I did not select was _____	One alternative I did not select was _____
"A Choice I Made"	"A Choice I Made"
I chose to _____	I chose to _____
One alternative I did not select was _____	One alternative I did not select was _____
"A Choice I Made"	"A Choice I Made"
I chose to _____	I chose to _____
One alternative I did not select was _____	One alternative I did not select was _____

HOMEGRAM 4

Dear Homework Helper,

Over the next few days, your student will be involved in classroom activities aimed at helping him or her learn about making choices. In connection with this classroom work, we have asked your student to carry out an activity at home, which will involve assuming the role of a teacher. The task will be to teach *you* what a choice is and to discuss with you some of your choices over the last few days. These choices do not have to be big ones. Something as simple as what you did to relax last evening will do. Your student is to make a list of the choices you discuss and bring this list to class. (A form for the list is provided on the attached page.)

In addition, he or she is to bring a "Choice Can" to class. This is simply a can (a soup can, for example) that has no rough edges and is covered with aluminum foil. We will use these cans in our classroom activities.

I appreciate your help with this assignment.

Sincerely,

My Homework Helper's Choices

_____   _____

_____   _____

_____   _____

_____   _____

Lesson 5
Opportunity Cost
What does a choice cost you?

Cognitive Objectives:

Students will

- Recognize that an alternative is given up when a choice is made.
- Define *opportunity cost*.
- Identify the opportunity cost of different decisions.

Affective Objectives:

Students will

- Recognize the importance of identifying the opportunity cost of a potential choice.
- Use the concept of *opportunity cost* before making decisions.
- Avoid using the word "free."

Service-learning Objective:

Students will

- Identify the opportunity cost of their service-learning choice.

Students who identify the opportunity cost of potential decisions think more carefully about whether the choice they are about to make is the best choice for them. People constantly make decisions about how to allocate their time, effort, and other resources to one activity as opposed to another. Young children may make the decision to spend time being with their friends, watching TV, playing a video game, reading, sleeping, doing homework, or any number of other activities. Having come this far in *Choices and Changes*, students should recognize now that deciding to do a certain thing has a cost. That cost is the opportunity to do something else—the next best alternative. At this point, the goal is to help the students identify and consider the cost they pay for a potential decision and to use that cost in weighing the advantages and disadvantages of alternatives.

It can be difficult for teachers and parents to accept the fact that the opportunity cost of a decision is subjective: it can be identified only by the decision-maker. Not grasping this point, some adults fall into the trap of trying to tell children what their opportunity cost is in a given case. A child who chooses to watch TV during the evening may be told, for example, that she wasted her time because she could have been doing her homework instead. That declaration assumes that the child would have done her homework if only she hadn't chosen to watch TV. But the child might not have settled on homework as her second-best choice. If she hadn't spent her time watching TV, she might have chosen to spend it talking to a friend on the telephone or playing video games or planning her weekend. Opportunity cost is what *the decision-maker* would have chosen as her next-best alternative, not what her teacher or parents would have liked her to choose.

But teachers and parents can help in these cases. They can help young people understand the value of the opportunities they forgo in the choices they make. Teachers can strive to help students see that taking school seriously now can yield benefits later in school and in life after school—benefits the students will forgo if they choose not to take school seriously. In this connection, the concept of opportunity cost can be a powerful motivator for students to develop skills and attitudes that will be valuable to them later.

Required Books

- *A Day's Work*
- *Big Squeak, Little Squeak*
- *Uncle Jed's Barbershop*

Optional Books

- *Grandfather's Journey*
- *How Many Days to America?*
- *Sam and the Lucky Money*
- *The Morning Chair*

Required Materials

- "Choice Cards": Four cards for each student or one page per student
- A piece of heavy paper for each student and some art supplies to enable the students to make a picture on both sides of the paper (a total of two pictures, one piece of paper)
- Poster board for a "No Free Lunch" sign and other signs

Economics Background for Teachers

Opportunity cost is the alternative that a person gives up in choosing one alternative over another. One of the most frequently quoted statements in economics is "There is no such thing as a free lunch." Students often want to challenge this statement, suggesting examples of things that do seem to be free. Unfortunately, the examples suggested usually illustrate the students' misunderstanding of the concept of cost.

Opportunity cost is the value of the next-best alternative a person gives up in making a decision. Notice the last part of the sentence: in making a decision. From an economist's perspective, *things* don't have costs, *decisions* do. This does not mean it is a bad thing to make decisions, nor does the opportunity cost in a given case mean that the decision in question is a bad one. It is simply an inescapable fact that choice always involves opportunity cost; you can't have one without the other.

When people choose, they select from a pool of potential alternatives. Once the list is narrowed to two alternatives, the person choosing selects one and gives up (declines to choose) the other. The alternative not chosen is the opportunity cost of the choice made. In *consumption* decisions (e.g., should we repair the clutch or get new brakes for the old car?), people decide how to allocate limited income. Even when decisions do not involve money, however, there is still an opportunity cost. Joe Dokes is offered three alternatives: a candy bar, an ice cream cone, or a soft drink. He thinks about which treat he'd prefer to have, and he narrows his range of choices down to the candy bar and the ice cream before choosing the ice cream. The opportunity cost of choosing the ice cream is the value of the candy bar (the enjoyment Joe would have derived from eating the candy bar) regardless of whether Joe paid for the item or not. Joe's choice came with an opportunity cost, as all choices do.

Production decisions (e.g., should we grow beets or carrots in the backyard vegetable garden?) also involve opportunity cost. When resources are allocated to produce education, for example, the cost of that choice is the best alternative use of those resources. As a teacher, you have skills and knowledge that could be used to do other things besides teaching school. The opportunity cost of your choice (to teach) is the best alternative use of your skills and knowledge. Every day that you decide to stay in teaching, you pay an opportunity cost–what you would be doing if you were not teaching. It might be retirement and spending time with grandchildren, staying home with a baby, working at an alternative job, or pure leisure. Only you can identify the opportunity cost of your decision to teach. Again, the fact that your decision to teach comes at a cost does not mean that the decision is a bad one. As long as the benefits of teaching, as you assess them, outweigh the value of your best alternative, the decision to teach is right for you.

The most important decisions schoolchildren make are likely to be ones about allocating themselves—their effort, their attachments to others, and so on. Each time they decide what to *do* in the daily run of events, they give up an opportunity to do something else—to grasp their next best alternative. On a Saturday afternoon, they may decide to go to a friend's birthday party rather than a movie. The decision obviously involves giving up the opportunity to see the movie, at least until another time. Other examples of this sort will come readily to mind, and in discussing them teachers can help students to see choices and alternatives where they might otherwise have supposed that events merely happened to them. (In pursuing such analyses, however, teachers should be mindful of parental restrictions as a factor limiting the alternatives available to students.)

In any choice among alternatives, the opportunity cost can be identified only when the range of alternatives has been narrowed to two. In considering a list of alternatives, people usually reject items on the list until they get down to two. Then they choose one and reject the other. The alternative selected is the choice; the one rejected is the opportunity cost.

The concept of opportunity cost explains one of the most famous statements in economics: "There is no such thing as a free lunch." All this statement means is that every choice has a cost. If someone offers to buy lunch at a restaurant for another person, the other person still doesn't get a free lunch; the choice to go to lunch (and not pay the tab) involves giving up an opportunity to do something else. Free lunches don't exist because every choice has a cost. One of the words that is not acceptable in economics is "free."

Vocabulary

- **Opportunity cost**: The value of the best alternative given up when a choice is made.

Getting Started

Remind the students that they have been learning about choices. Today they will learn about an important consequence of choices—the opportunity cost that comes with every choice. Write the term "Opportunity Cost" on the board. Underneath it write four statements: "To Choose Is to Refuse," "Opportunity Cost Is Opportunity Lost," "Every Choice Has a Cost," and "Things Don't Have Costs, Choices Do." As you write each statement, read it to the students. Tell them they will learn more about opportunity cost and the meaning of these statements in today's lesson. What they learn may help them to plan their service-learning project.

Teaching Procedures

1. Read *Uncle Jed's Barbershop*. Ask the students to identify some important decisions that Uncle Jed made. (*Answers might include cutting people's hair even if they didn't have money, saving to buy a barbershop, using his money for Sarah Jean's operation, saving again after choosing to use the money for the operation, saving again after he lost his money during the depression, buying his barbershop at last.*)

2. Tell the children that you want to discuss the decision to pay for Sarah Jean's operation. Ask the following question:

• What alternative use did Uncle Jed have for the money? (*He could have used the money for the barbershop.*)

In discussing the students' answers, explain that the best alternative given up in making a decision is called the opportunity cost. Refer to the term on the board. When Uncle Jed chose to use his money for Sarah Jean's operation, the cost of the operation was not the money; the cost was what Uncle Jed might otherwise have done with that money. When he chose to use the money for the operation, he gave up his best alternative use of the money—that is, the barbershop.

3. Next, turn to the four statements on the board. Read them and explain them by reference to Uncle Jed's decision. Explain that Uncle Jed's choice *cost* him his barbershop; the barbershop was his "opportunity lost."

4. Ask the students if they think Uncle Jed had carefully considered the opportunity cost of his decision to use his money for the operation. (*Yes, he did. He says in the story that "money didn't matter. He couldn't let anything happen to his Sarah Jean."*)

5. Read *A Day's Work*.

• Ask the students to identify Francisco's choices. (*Answers will include going to look for work with Abuelo, going to the job with Abuelo, lying to Mr. Benjamin, pushing the guy in the van, working with Abuelo.*)

- Ask the students to identify Abuelo's choices. (*Answers will include coming to the United States to help his daughter and her family, looking for work, working, working on Sunday to make up for the mistake.*)
- Ask the students to identify the opportunity cost of Abuelo's decision to work on Sunday. (*This will be difficult since we don't know Abuelo, but the opportunity cost might be Sunday Mass.*)
- Ask the students when Francisco chooses to go with Abuelo on Sunday, what is the opportunity cost of that decision? (*The Lakers game. Some students will say that Francisco had no choice—that he had to go with Abuelo—but that is not the case. Francisco could have refused to go. The consequences might have included the day in his room or other punishment, but he did make a choice, and the opportunity cost of the choice was the Lakers game. Note: you may have to specify that Mom does not have a VCR so she could not tape the game. Also be careful about Abuelo's statement that the Lakers game is the price of the lie. The game is not the opportunity cost of the choice to lie since Francisco did not know he would have to give up the game when he chose to lie. Opportunity cost is the value of the best-known alternative.*)

6. If you use *Grandfather's Journey,* ask the following questions.

- What choices did Grandfather make? (*He chose to come to America; then he chose to return to Japan.*)
- What was the opportunity cost of Grandfather's decision to go to America? (*Being in Japan.*) What was the opportunity cost of his decision to return to Japan? (*Being in California.*)
- What is the significance of the sentence, "The funny thing is, the moment I am in one country, I am homesick for the other"? (*Every decision has a cost. The fact that we choose the best alternative doesn't mean that we don't want the next best alternative.*)

7. If you use *The Morning Chair,* explain that Bram's parents had asked the question, "Where shall we live?" and had narrowed their alternatives down to two: Holland or America. Ask the following questions.

- What were the things Bram missed about Holland? (*The brick house, friendly neighbors, walks with Papa to the sea, his clackety scooter, his little bed with the straw mattress, Oma's quilt, and time with Mama in the morning chair.*)
- What were the benefits of being in America? (*Sunday walks with his parents in the park, hot dogs, the birds, the teeter-totter, policemen on horses.*)
- What parts of Holland did Bram get to take to America with him? (*His bed, Oma's quilt, the morning chair.*)
- What was the opportunity cost of choosing America? (*Being in Holland.*)

8. If you use *Sam and the Lucky Money*, ask the following questions.

• What were the alternatives Sam had for using his money? *(Be sure the answers include giving the money to the old man. If students suggest that he might have bought a basketball, include that answer on the board, but later remind the students that the alternatives must be realistic. Sam couldn't buy a basketball with four dollars.)*

• If the students were Sam, what would they do with the money if they did not give it to the old man? *(Answers will vary.)* Explain that that alternative that they would have chosen if they didn't give the money to the old man is their opportunity cost.

9. Have the students complete a report card for any of the characters in the stories above. The Report Card is found in Activity 3-1.

10. Read *Big Squeak, Little Squeak*. Before reading the story, write the word "FREE" on the board. Have the students repeat the word, and explain to them that every choice has an opportunity cost; thus no choice is free. Tell them that "free" is not a word that can be used in this class. Tell them to look for the word "free" in the story and to point it out to you when they see it. *(The word appears on the cheese in the cat's store.)* Ask the students why they think the cat puts that word on the cheese. *(To lure the mice into the store.)* The word next appears on the sign outside the dog's store advertising "free" catnip. Ask the students why they think the dog uses the word. *(To lure the cat into the store.)* Generalize that the word "free" usually means something else and is often used to deceive people.

11. Tell the students that you want them to draw two pictures. The pictures may be of any of the characters in any of the books they have read for this lesson. Because resources are limited, each student will have only one piece of paper to use, but they may use both sides. When the pictures are complete, ask each student to choose one of the two to be displayed on the bulletin board. This picture should be labeled with the word "CHOICE." The other picture should be labeled with the words "OPPORTUNITY COST." Tell the students that you will display their choice on the bulletin board. The opportunity cost will not be displayed since you can't display both pictures at once. The picture they gave up when they labeled it "OPPORTUNITY COST" is the cost of their choice. (A good time to do this activity is just before a parents' night.)

12. Ask the students the following questions. Why couldn't they have two pieces of paper? *(Scarcity.)* What two alternatives did they have? *(The two pictures they drew.)* What was their choice? What was the opportunity cost of their choice? *(The picture they chose not to put up.)*

13. Explain that every choice has an opportunity cost, and that it is important to identify the cost of a decision before making the decision.

Assessment

1. Distribute a copy of the four choice cards found at the end of this lesson to each student. (An alternative is to project a transparency of each situation on the overhead. The advantage of the cards is that every student does the exercise independently.) Ask the students to look at the choice cards they have been given. For the situation on each card, have them limit the alternatives to their favorite two; then they should identify a choice and identify the opportunity cost.

2. Ask the students to explain how each of these statements describes opportunity cost.

- "To choose is to refuse." *(When a person makes a choice, he or she refuses the opportunity cost.)*
- "Opportunity cost is opportunity lost." *(When a person selects one alternative, he or she gives up the next best opportunity.)*
- "Every choice has a cost." *(When a person selects an alternative, the cost he or she pays is the next best alternative.)*
- "There is no such thing as a free lunch." *(When a person makes a choice, he or she pays an opportunity cost even if no money is involved.)*

Have the students make "signs" of these statements and put them on the walls around the room.

Follow Through

When appropriate, help the students identify the opportunity cost of their decisions before they make them. Never allow them to use the word "free" without a comment about opportunity cost. They will catch you once in a while, and that will help them recognize that even adults make that mistake from time to time.

Optional Activity

If you are planning a forthcoming unit on immigration, use the concepts of *goals, alternatives, advantages and disadvantages, choice* and *opportunity cost* to investigate the immigration of different groups of people to the United States. Ask the students to speak to their Homework Helpers about their own family origins, when family members first came to America, why, and what they left behind. Then have the students discuss the opportunity cost of their family members' immigrant choices. In many cases, people came to America because the opportunity cost was pretty low. This point is illustrated in *How Many Days to America?* If the students can obtain the necessary information, ask them what their immigrant relatives thought the advantages of America would be and whether their hopes were realized.

Choice Cards

Grandpa sent you birthday money. You have a lot of things that you could do with it. Your mother wants you to put the money in the bank for your college fund. Your best friend wants you to go halves on a computer program that you can both use. Your brother said you should spend the money when the family goes on vacation. You were thinking of treating yourself to a great meal at a fast food place. What are your two best alternatives? What are the advantages and disadvantages of each? What do you choose? What is the opportunity cost of your choice?	At recess you have many things that you could do. A friend wants you to play kickball with him. Another friend wants you to play tetherball. Your teacher said he would help you with a class assignment that you missed. You were thinking about playing a video game. What are your two best alternatives? What are the advantages and disadvantages of each? What do you choose? What is the opportunity cost of your choice?
After school you could do your homework, play with friends, watch TV, play a computer game, or sleep. What are your two best alternatives? What are the advantages and disadvantages of each? What do you choose? What is the opportunity cost of your choice?	Your mom is buying your school clothes. You see a great pair of shoes that cost a lot of money. You can get the shoes, but if you do, you won't be able to buy the shirt, hat, and pants that you really should have for school. What are the benefits and costs of the shoes or the shirt, hat, and pants? What do you choose? What is the opportunity cost of your choice?

Lesson 6
Decision Making
How do you make decisions?

Cognitive Objectives:

Students will

- Define *decision making*.
- Identify a goal.
- Use five steps to make a decision.

Affective Objectives:

Students will

- Use the decision-making process in their lives.
- Use step 5 to re-evaluate their decisions, including decisions about how to treat others.
- Learn that practicing helps them make more informed decisions.

Students will learn that making decisions without thinking them through and collecting sufficient information can lead to consequences they did not anticipate. They will learn to find out about others before they decide how to treat them. They will learn the importance of stopping to reconsider a decision in cases in which new information relevant to that decision comes to light.

Service-learning Objective:

Students will

- Use a five-step decision-making process to choose a service-learning project.

Required Books

- *Brandi's Braids*
- *Chicken Sunday*
- *No Plain Pets*
- *The King, the Mice, and the Cheese*

Optional Books

- *Old Henry*
- *Angel Child, Dragon Child*
- *The Raft*
- *Lily's Purple Plastic Purse*
- *A Present for Toot*
- *The Woman Who Outshone the Sun*

Required Materials

- The Decision-Making Apron
- Decision Cards
- Small pieces of paper or 3″ × 5″ cards
- *Student Journal,* pages 6-1 and 6-2

Optional Materials

- Quilt-making materials for optional activity
- The following books if you choose the optional quilting activity:
  Eight Hands Round
  Sweet Clara and the Freedom Quilt
  The Keeping Quilt
  The Patchwork Quilt

Economics Background for Teachers

In this lesson, which concludes Unit 1, students make use of their learning from Lessons 1-5, developing and applying their decision-making skills. When people choose, they view a group of alternatives and select one from among the best two. The alternative that they select is their choice. The process of selecting this choice is called decision making.

The decision-making process can be described by reference to five steps:

1. State the goal.
2. Identify the alternatives.
3. List the advantages and disadvantages of each alternative, recognizing that the best alternative not chosen will be the opportunity cost of the choice.
4. Decide.
5. Re-evaluate (decide whether the choice was a good one).

Students have seen each of these steps in isolation, except for step 5. This lesson engages students with all five steps.

Vocabulary

- **Decision making**: The process of selecting choices.
- **Goal**: Something that a person wants to have or do.
- **Re-evaluate**: To think again about a decision made previously.

Getting Started

Explain to the students that they have been discussing choices and changes for a while now. Today is a big day because they are going to use what they have learned so far to develop a way of making decisions in an organized manner. They will learn five steps to use in making decisions, and they will use those steps to select their service-learning project. (Note: Since this lesson concludes Unit 1, it will require more than one class period for completion.)

Teaching Procedures

1. Write the term "decision making" on the board. Explain that decision making is a process to follow in evaluating alternatives and selecting choices. Tell them that you are going to read a story in which people don't seem to be thinking about the decisions they make.

2. Read and discuss *The King, the Mice, and the Cheese*. This is a story about a king who has some cheese that a group of mice keep eating. The king asks his advisors what to do, and they suggest getting some cats. The cats chase away the mice, but they also take over the palace, so now the king is stuck with a new problem. The advisors suggest getting some dogs. The dogs chase the cats away, but they also take over. The process continues until the king invites the mice back and makes a deal with them; he will share his cheese if they will behave properly.

- Ask the students if they think the king's advisors did their job properly. (*They didn't advise the king very well. The story illustrates poor decision making.*)

- Ask the students to re-enact the story. One student should play the king and different students should play the role of advisor for each decision (e.g., get cats, get dogs, etc.) Stop the action after each advisor has presented her or his suggestion and have the class identify some disadvantages that the advisors did not consider.

3. Put on the decision-making apron or go to the wall where the decision-making poster is attached or project the decision-making apron transparency on the overhead. Tell the students that a goal is something you want to do or have or be. A goal may be finding the best way to overcome an obstacle, or the best thing to do with a $25 birthday present, or the best way to spend a Saturday afternoon, or the best way to save money for college. Right now, the students are going to pretend to be an advisor to a little boy who wants a pet. They are going to help the boy decide what type of pet to get. Explain that the goal of the process is to find a suitable pet for the boy.

- Read *No Plain Pets.* The story describes a group of pets that a boy wants; most of these pets are not easy to maintain.
- Ask the students to list some pets that they might want. *(The list will probably include cat, dog, bird, fish, snake, hamster, and others.)* Break the students up into groups of two or three and have each group narrow the list of pets to two. Then have the students list the advantages and disadvantages of each pet listed. *(Considerations should include the purchase price of the pet, the costs of maintaining it, how much care it would take, how big it would get, whether their parents would approve, whether they could have it in their house if they are renting, and others.)*
- Have each group decide what type of pet they would choose and what their opportunity cost would be.

4. Distribute paper and crayons or other drawing tools.

- Ask the students to draw pictures of the goal. (The goal is to have a pet that would be best for them.) When they have finished with the pictures, place them in the first pocket of the decision-making apron labeled GOAL.
- Have the students do the same (draw pictures) with the two alternative pets, identified by the groups in procedure 3. Then have them list the advantages and disadvantages of each alternative.
- Finally, have the students draw pictures of their choice and place them in the apron. Explain that they have just used four of the five decision-making steps.
- List these steps on the board.
  Step 1: State the goal.
  Step 2: Identify the alternatives.

Step 3: List the advantages and disadvantages of each alternative.

Step 4: Choose, and consider the opportunity cost of the choice.

5. Tell the students that they are going to identify a choice. Read *Brandi's Braids*. After you have finished reading, ask the following questions.

- What decisions did Brandi's mother make? *(She decided to sell her hair; she decided to let the barber buy Brandi's hair.)*
- What decision did Brandi make? *(She decided to offer her hair. Explain to the children that selling hair was a big sacrifice because people knew that women with short hair were very poor.)*
- What were the first four steps of the decision-making process for Brandi? *(The hardest part of this exercise is identifying alternatives. Brandi's mother wanted a new net so that she could continue fishing to earn a living. While there may have been some alternatives to selling hair, they were few and less desirable than selling hair. Brandi's mother could have decided to give up and become a beggar, for example. To say that people have alternatives is not always to say that they have attractive, desirable alternatives.)*

6. Explain to the children that people often change their minds after making a choice because they see the consequences of their choices and realize that the alternative they have chosen may not have been the best one. This is particularly true in decisions people make about other people. Read *Chicken Sunday*, and then ask the following questions.

- What was Mr. Kodinski's original opinion about the children? *(He thought they were nasty because they threw eggs at him.)*
- Did he gather information before choosing to dislike the children? *(No.)*
- What did Miss Eula choose to believe? *(The children were telling the truth.)*
- What was the children's goal? *(They wanted to find a way to change Mr. Kodinski's mind about them.)*
- What alternative did they select to achieve their goal? *(They decided to make some decorated eggs for him.)*
- How did Mr. Kodinski react to their gift? *(He re-evaluated his opinion about the children.)*
- What did the children decide to do to earn the money for Miss Eula's hat? *(They made Ukranian Easter eggs and sold them in Mr. Kodinski's store.)*

7. In each of the optional books listed above, characters re-evaluate their original decisions about people or activities. Ask the students to review why the characters made their original decisions; then ask them to review the additional information that helped them to rethink their decisions.

8. Write the fifth step of the decision-making process on the board.

   Step 5: Re-evaluate the decision.

9. Have the students turn to page 6-1 in their journals. Ask them to use one of the stories they have read for this lesson and to analyze a decision one of the characters has made, using the five steps of the decision-making process. To assess this activity, look for the following:
   a. Is the goal correctly identified?
   b. Has the student identified two alternatives from the story?
   c. Is there some indication of the advantages and disadvantages of each alternative?
   d. Has the student chosen one of the two alternatives? Is the opportunity cost identified?

Service Learning Project

Put on the decision-making apron or go to the poster on the bulletin board or use the apron transparency. Tell the students that they are now going to use the five steps to decide on their service-learning project. The goal is to identify a service-learning project. The alternatives are those that have been discussed. Have them list the two alternatives that they have proposed and review the advantages and disadvantages of both possibilities. Have them vote on the projects. Once the choice has been identified, tell the students that they have selected their service-learning project carefully. Nonetheless, they will have an opportunity to rethink their decision at a later point in the *Choices and Changes* program to see if they still think their decision is a good one.

Have the students turn to page 6-2 in their journals. Ask them to answer the questions on the page, thus describing how they selected their service-learning project.

Optional Activity

Help the children make a quilt that represents the steps they took to make a decision concerning the service-learning project. The quilt can be as simple as white cardboard squares upon which the children draw the steps of the decision-making process. There should be pictures of the goal (to do something helpful for the school or an individual), the alternatives they considered, the benefits and costs of those alternatives, and their choice. You could put the choice in the middle, with alternatives surrounding it, or the goal in the middle with alternatives surrounding it, or follow any other design the children develop. The squares can be hole-punched in each corner and tied together with colored yarn. Or the class can make a cloth quilt, with help from you or a quilt maker from your school or community. Instructions for a cloth quilt can be found at the end of this lesson. When you complete your service-learning project, the class can present the quilt to the individual or organization for whom the project was done. Parents and the principal can be invited to this presentation. (Students this age like this project. You might want to consider making a quilt as a service-learning project. One idea is to have the class "interview" an elderly individual or couple, asking them to tell about their lives. The quilt can then be a history of the individual's or couple's life, with drawings depicting stories they have told the class. Or use *Eight Hands Round* to make an alphabet quilt for your class or for a younger class. If you choose to make a quilt, look ahead to Lesson 12 to help the children understand that they need a plan for production.)

Most communities have a quilting society. Check with the city library or look for the American Quilter's Society (AQS) on the web (http://www.aqsquilt.com/) or call (270-898-7903) to identify a guild near you.

If you decide to make a quilt, you can read the books for the optional activity listed above.

Assessment

Use the decision-making process to identify a choice from the Decision Cards provided at the end of this lesson.

Follow Through

Encourage the students to continue using the five-step decision-making process. From time to time when the class is to make an important decision, put on the decision-making apron or go to the decision-making poster or use the apron transparency and lead the children through the first four steps. Where appropriate, revisit the decision later with step five.

STUDENT JOURNAL Page 6-1

A Decision

1. What was the character trying to do? What was the goal?

2. What were some of the alternatives?

3. What were the advantages and disadvantages of some of the alternatives?

4. What do you think were the two best alternatives?

5. What alternative did the character choose?

6. What was the opportunity cost of the decision?

STUDENT JOURNAL Page 6-2
Our Service-Learning Decision

1. What was the question that we had to answer?

2. What were our two best alternatives?

3. What were the advantages and disadvantages of the two alternatives?

4. Which did we choose? What was the opportunity cost of our decision?

Optional Activity

Directions for Making A Simple Tie-Quilt

1. Cut 49 6×6 inch squares.
2. Arrange squares in 7 horizontal rows, each containing 7 squares.
3. Stitch squares together by matching right sides. When completed, you will have 7 rows of squares.
4. Stitch rows together vertically to make a square that measures approximately 42×42 inches.
5. Cut a 42×42 inch backing of cotton or muslin.
6. Placing right sides together, stitch around the quilt. Leave an opening of approximately 18 inches on one side for stuffing.
7. Turn the quilt right side out and press.
8. Cut a piece of quilter's batting the size of the finished quilt.
9. Layer the batting between the top and bottom of the quilt.
10. Hand stitch the opening closed.
11. Using a 12-inch length of embroidery thread, tie each corner of each square. Make certain that the stitch secures both the top and the bottom of the quilt. Make certain that each tie is knotted. Trim the excess thread.

Decision Cards

You have some homework due tomorrow. You can do it after school or tonight.	Your grandparents send you $20 for your birthday. What will you do with it?
You see a friend take something that doesn't belong to him/her.	It is Saturday morning. You usually mow the lawn for an older couple that lives down the street. This is the only time you can do it, and you would really like to sleep for another hour instead of getting up to mow the lawn.
You and your little sister are home alone after school. She wants you to help her with her homework but you would like to play with your friends.	While riding your bike, you find a wallet. There is money inside and also an ID with an address. What do you do?
Mom has told you not to play ball in the house. One afternoon you toss your ball and it knocks a lamp over and breaks it.	You get to choose what your family is going to do on Friday night–order pizza and rent a movie, go out for fast food and a movie, or go out for fast food and bowling.

You are in the grocery store. You have $2.00. What do you do with your money?	You are supposed to bake something for a school project. What do you bake?
There is a substitute teacher in your classroom. Other kids in the class are not following the class rules and are misbehaving. What do you do?	Your best friend asks you to spend the night and you agree. Then another friend asks you to have dinner at his house. You really want to have dinner at the other friend's house.
A group of your friends start picking on a student who doesn't have many friends. You want to help him, but you are afraid of what the other kids might think.	You really want to have a new bike that is expensive. You have some money saved, and your mom said she will pay half but you have to pay the other half. You see a video game that you really want.
You finish your homework early. You are reading a great book, your favorite TV show is on, and you have a new computer game. What do you do?	A kid is picking on you and taking your lunch money.

Your best friend wants you to let him copy the answers to the math assignment. He says he didn't have time to do the assignment himself.	You are the captain for picking teams for kickball in P.E. Your best friend is not very good.
You are in the middle of making cookies and you don't have enough eggs. What do you do?	You are home alone and someone knocks on the door. Your mom told you not to let anyone in.
You see lots of bruises on your friend and you are worried about him. He says he fell down, but you have seen bruises many times.	A cat has babies in your yard. She is wild and runs away when you go outside. You find the babies and they're really cute. What do you do?
You and your sisters are supposed to do some chores. You do yours, but your sisters don't do their part. Mom expects the chores to be done when she gets home.	You are skateboarding with friends. You find a downhill street that would be really fun to go down, but there is an intersection at the bottom. Your friend goes down and then dares you to go.

You chew gum on the way to school and forget to take it out before going into class. You remember when you sit down and class is starting. You are not allowed to get out of your seat during this time.	You went camping over the weekend. When you get to class Monday morning and begin taking your books out of your backpack you notice that you forgot to remove your pocketknife from the pack before coming to school. The pocketknife is not allowed on school property.

UNIT TWO

WORK, SCHOOL, AND MY HUMAN CAPITAL

UNIT TWO
Overview: Work, School, and My Human Capital

Unit 2 introduces students to the nature and characteristics of goods and services and work and workers. Students are encouraged to view themselves as workers and the activities that they do in school as work. They learn that they are a powerful bundle of human capital and that the work they do in school is an investment in their human capital. They learn that they are responsible for their education, the only ones who can decide whether their human capital will increase or not.

Lesson 7. Goods and Services, Work and Workers

Students read a variety of books that acquaint them with the concepts of work and workers. They identify goods and services and particular work and workers and help a fictional character named Alvin identify workers that he sees.

Lesson 8. The Work I Do

Students read from a list of books. They identify the work that they do at home and the work that they do in school. They decorate and wear worker identification cards and begin to keep track of the work they do at school and at home.

Lesson 9. I Am a Bundle of Human Capital

Students read a variety of books to identify useful skills. They learn that human capital consists of skills and knowledge. They prepare a skills inventory to help them identify the skills that they possess. They use a "Can Do Can" to visualize the skills that they acquire.

Lesson 10. School Is an Investment in Human Capital

In this lesson students make the connection between the work that they do in school and their opportunities in later life. They read *More Than Anything Else* and *Richard Wright and the Library Card* to discover that reading and other skills learned in school improve both the quantity and the quality of alternatives available to them in later life. This lesson also helps students understand the power of reading.

Lesson 7
Goods and Services, Work and Workers

What are goods and services? What is work?

Cognitive Objectives:

Students will

- Distinguish between *goods* and *services*.
- Define *work* as physical or mental effort from which a good or service is produced.
- Identify different types of work.
- Identify *workers* as people who produce goods and services.

Affective Objectives:

Students will

- Develop an awareness of the work around them.

Both men and women do work and it is done in the home and outside the home. In this lesson, students begin to understand and value work in all of its forms.

Required Books

- One or more of the following:
  Career Day
  Carolina Shout
  Daddies at Work
  Learning is Fun with Mrs. Perez
  Mommies at Work

Mothers Can Do Anything
New Cat
Riding the School Bus with Mrs. Kramer
Who Uses This?
Work Song

Required Materials

- *Student Journal,* pages 7-1 through 7-7
- Homegram 7
- Activity 7-1

Economics Background for Teachers

Goods are *things* that are produced or made; they are objects people can use to satisfy their wants. Services are *actions* that can satisfy a person's wants. Work is human effort used to produce goods or services. Workers are people who work. Work can be done inside the home or outside the home. It can be done for others or for oneself. It can be for pay or not for pay.

Vocabulary

- **Good**: An object that can be used to satisfy a person's wants.
- **Service**: An action that can satisfy a person's wants.
- **Work**: Human physical or mental effort used in production of goods or services.
- **Worker**: A person who does work.

Getting Started

Tell the students that they have been learning how to make decisions. Today they are going to learn about goods and services and work, so that they can begin to make decisions about work.

Teaching Procedures

1. Write the words "goods" and "services" on the board. Discuss the definitions of goods and services. *(A good is an object that can be used to satisfy a person's wants. A service is an action that can satisfy a person's wants.)* Help the students distinguish between goods and services, using examples. *(Apples, bananas, books, cars, and computers are all examples of goods. Teaching, dentistry, fighting fires, and providing health care are all examples of services.)* Have the students turn to page 7-1 in their journals and identify goods and services.

2. Write the words "work" and "worker" on the board. Ask the students what work is. Entertain their answers, encouraging them to think about many different kinds of work. Tell them even though we all think we know what work is, there is more to it than most of us realize. Write on the board and discuss the following points about work:

   a. Work is human effort used in the production of goods or services. It can involve physical effort, thinking, or both.
   b. A worker is a person who does work.
   c. Work can be done at school, in the home, or outside the home.

3. Draw three columns on the board or use the transparency master **Activity 7-1**, with the headings **Good, Service,** and **Worker**. Tell the students that you are going to read a story or stories to them and you would like them to raise their hands any time they hear something that can fit into any of the three columns on the board or overhead. To complete the three columns they should identify products as falling into the good or service category, and in each case they should tell what the worker is called. For example, a person who works on your teeth provides a service and might be called a dentist or a dental hygienist. Read any or all of the books listed in the **Required Materials** section. (*Mommies at Work* is the only one that depicts work done at home, so you probably should include it in your reading to the class.) When you have completed the reading, discuss the three columns with the children, being sure that they understand the difference between a good and a service and that they can identify workers and the work they do.

4. Have the students turn to pages 7-2 and 7-3 in their journals.

• Ask them to identify and discuss each of the figures on the pages. Encourage them to share their knowledge of people who do jobs like the ones shown in the pictures. After each figure has been identified, ask the students what all the people portrayed have in common. Help them to conclude that the people all do work (carpenter, barber, mail carrier, taxi driver, firefighter, TV news reporter, shoe salesman, artist, server, doctor).
• Point out that both students and adults work. Point to the word "work" on the board and ask the students to identify work that they see done at home (cooking, cleaning, and taking care of children, for example). Who are the workers at school, and what work do they do? (teachers/teaching, custodians/cleaning, cafeteria workers/cooking in the cafeteria, principals/administering, office workers/typing, filing, making phone calls, etc.)

5. (For kindergarten and first grade) Read *Who Uses This?* Have the students answer the questions in the book. Write the name of the tool and the name of the

worker on the board. Ask the students to think of other tools that specific workers use. Write the names of these tools and the workers on the board also.

6. (Optional) Encourage the students to identify other examples of goods and services by making up riddles about workers for classmates to guess. In their riddles students should tell if the worker produces a good or performs a service; they should also give hints about the good or service. The riddles may be rhyming or non-rhyming. Example: I make goods. The goods I make are made of wood. They hold books. Who am I? Answer: A carpenter who makes bookshelves.

Assessment

Have the students turn to **Alvin's Homework** in their journals, beginning at page 7-4. Explain that this comics-style journal entry features Alvin, a child about their age, who has a problem. Challenge them to help Alvin solve his problem. Be sure the students are familiar with the format of comics and know how to follow the frames to read the story. Show them that the words in the boxes within the frames explain the action in the story. The sentences in the "balloons" tell what people are saying; those in wavy-line "balloons" (the first frame) tell what people are thinking. If the students are able to read the story, you may have them take turns reading the frames or appoint various students to read the people parts and the action boxes. You may wish to read the story to them first, and then have them read it a second time through.

Tell the students they can help Alvin with his homework by going back through the story to identify workers. Have the students identify a partner or small group with whom they will work. Explain that their task will be to list all 12 workers in the story. One student might write the names as another identifies and spells them. Workers should be identified by their jobs rather than their names (for example, "teacher" rather than "Mr. Thomas"). Students should identify the workers Alvin sees as well as those with whom he speaks. Direct them to list the workers on page 7-7 of their journals. Point out that each frame has one worker. (Workers from the story are a teacher, custodian, cook, bus driver, welder, lawyer, scientist, nurse, butcher, grocer, baker, and sitter.)

When all the students have finished, call on one group to read its list to the class. Instruct the others to check off the workers on their lists as the group that reads names them. As they finish, ask if any have workers on their lists not already identified. (Note: Sharing answers allows the students to check their work and to contribute to the class.)

Ask the groups to look again at the list of workers from **Alvin's Homework**. Have them work together to decide whether each worker is making a good or providing a service. Have them write **G** for good or **S** for service beside the name of each worker. When all the students have finished, review their answers. *(The baker and cook produce goods; the welder is helping to make a good—a building. All the rest of the workers provide services.)*

Follow Through

Read *Career Day*. From time to time arrange with parents or other adults to visit the class and describe the work that they do.

Homegram

Distribute *Homegram 7* and ask the students to take it home and give it to their Homework Helper.

Activity 7-1

GOOD	SERVICE	WORKER

STUDENT JOURNAL Page 7-1

Goods And Services

Goods are things that are produced or made, such as cars, bread, jeans, and houses.

A **service** is something a worker does for someone else, such as teaching, repairing, cleaning, and cutting hair.

Draw a circle around the pictures showing goods. Draw a line below the pictures showing services.

STUDENT JOURNAL Page 7-2

Workers, Workers, Workers

STUDENT JOURNAL Page 7-3

Workers, Workers, Workers

STUDENT JOURNAL Page 7-4

Alvin's Homework

STUDENT JOURNAL Page 7-5

Alvin's Homework

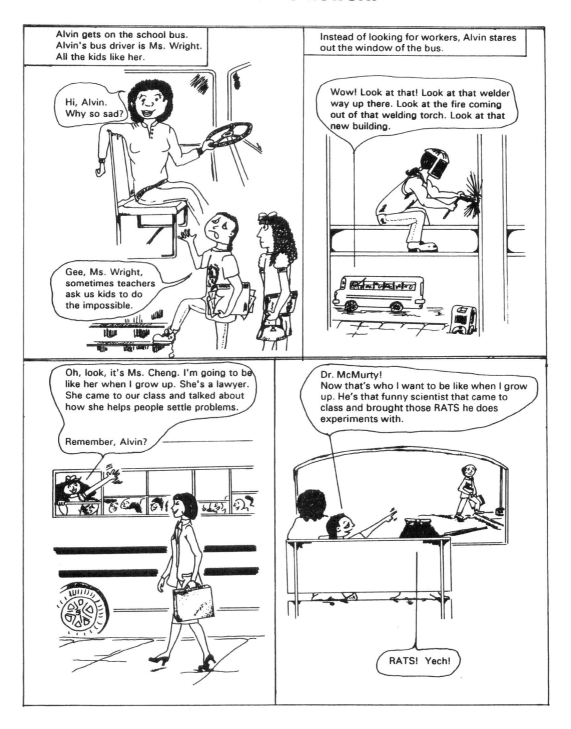

STUDENT JOURNAL Page 7-6

Alvin's Homework

STUDENT JOURNAL Page 7-7

Alvin's Homework

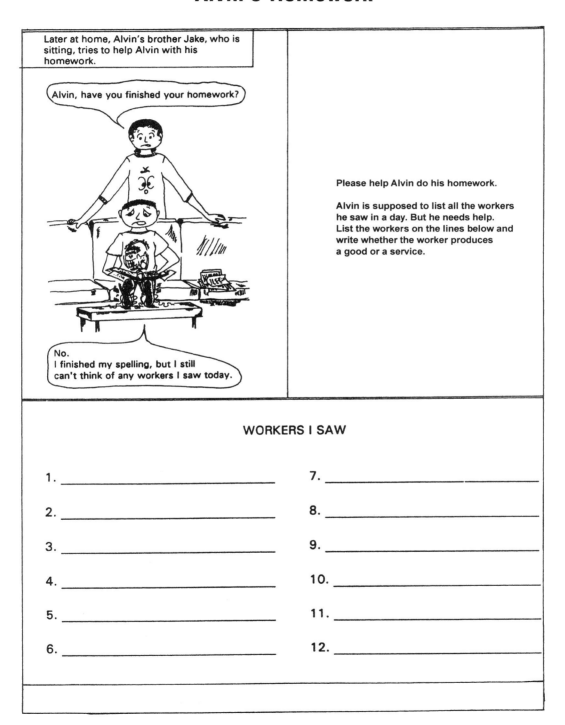

Later at home, Alvin's brother Jake, who is sitting, tries to help Alvin with his homework.

Alvin, have you finished your homework?

No.
I finished my spelling, but I still can't think of any workers I saw today.

Please help Alvin do his homework.

Alvin is supposed to list all the workers he saw in a day. But he needs help. List the workers on the lines below and write whether the worker produces a good or a service.

WORKERS I SAW

1. _____
2. _____
3. _____
4. _____
5. _____
6. _____

7. _____
8. _____
9. _____
10. _____
11. _____
12. _____

HOMEGRAM 7

Dear Homework Helper,

Today we learned about goods and services and work and workers. The children identified the type of work that many different people do both inside and outside the home. It would be helpful if you would discuss the concept of work with your student, explaining the type of work that you do, either inside or outside the home. Also, please help your student identify workers as you move around your neighborhood. People at the movies, grocery store, or gas station are all workers.

Thank you.

_____

Lesson 8
The Work I Do
What work do I do?

Cognitive Objectives:

Students will

- Identify work that they do at home and at school.
- Develop an awareness of themselves as workers.

Affective Objectives:

Students will

- Appreciate the work that they do in school.
- Take pride in their work.

Too often, children don't understand why they are in school. They begin to think about this more as they grow older. In this lesson, children learn that their activities in school are work, and their work is as important as work done by adults.

Required Books

One of the following:

- *Gator Cleans House*
- *Pigsty*
- *What Have You Done, Davy?*
- *Mel's Diner*

Optional Books

- *Just for You*
- *Just Me and My Dad*
- *Only Opa*
- *Time to Go*

Required Materials

- *Student Journal*, pages 8-1, 8-2, 8-3
- *Homegram 8*
- Worker Identification Cards, duplicated and cut apart to provide one per student
- Crayons or colored marking pens
- Large safety pins (one per student) or lengths of yarn (about 18″ each; one per student) or plastic badge holders
- Five (5) copies of Student Journal page 8-3 for each student

Optional Materials

- Camera and film

Economics Background for Teachers

Work is physical or mental effort used in the production of goods or services. Learning can be both physical and mental effort that produces human capital. Students will learn about human capital in the next lesson. Here, the major point is that school activities are physical and mental effort. The connection to human capital will be made in the next lesson.

Vocabulary

- **Work**: Human physical or mental effort used in production of goods and services.
- **Worker:** A person who does work.

Getting Started

Tell the students that they have learned about goods and services, work and workers. They used the story about Alvin's homework to identify particular workers and their work. Point out that the story also depicts another important person who is a worker, even though he is young and is not paid. That worker is

Alvin, and his job is to be a student. Tell them that each of them is also a worker at school and at home.

Teaching Procedures

1. Read one of the following: *Gator Cleans House, Pigsty, What Have You Done, Davy?* or *Mel's Diner.*

2. In discussing the story, ask the students to review things that the characters did, listing those actions that could be called work. (*In* Gator Cleans House, *the characters mopped, swept, vacuumed, polished, dusted, moved furniture, cleaned the tub, washed and dried the dishes, took out the garbage, and made the beds. In* Pigsty, *the characters swept, scoured, polished, and scrubbed. In* What Have You Done, Davy?, *Davy made new fir-cone animals for Daisy, built a playhouse with Donny, helped dig out Dan's burrow, and picked blueberries with his mother. In* Mel's Diner, *the young girl sets silverware on the tables, helps to make coffee, brings menus to customers, serves food, fills sugar bowls and napkin holders, keeps the glass by the cash register full of toothpicks, talks to customers, and listens.*) Explain to the students that each of these activities is work. People work at home as well as outside the home. Explain that everything the characters did was valued by themselves and others.

3. Ask the students why they think most people work. If they say "for money," agree that people are paid for work they do at their jobs, but note on the chalkboard examples of work for which people do not receive money, such as work done in the home (cooking, washing the dishes, mopping the floors, taking out the trash, feeding the pets). Explain that some nonpaying work is necessary for the day-to-day functioning of life. Also, some people do work for other people because it makes them feel good about themselves.

4. Have the students turn to page 8-1 in their journals and review the definition of "work" with them. Draw their attention to the bottom of the page and have them draw a picture of work that makes them feel good, even if they are not paid for it. Encourage the students to share ideas about the work they depict. (*Examples might be cooking, babysitting, studying spelling words, doing math, writing letters, or shopping.*)

5. Point out that in addition to the work the students have illustrated, they also do other work, at home and in school. Have them turn to page 8-2 in their journals and write down as many types of work as they can think of under the headings "At Home" and "At School." You may wish to discuss this activity initially with the whole class, recording students' ideas about other work they do on the chalkboard;

then individual students could copy ideas that apply to them in their journals. As an alternative, you might have the students complete this page in pairs, in small groups, or as homework.

6. Distribute Activity 8-1, containing the Worker Identification Cards. Give one card to each student. Ask the students if they have seen adults in some jobs wearing identification badges or cards. Tell the students that these cards show that the people are workers in those jobs. Have the students fill in their names, the school's name, and their job title (student) on their cards. Encourage them to decorate their identification cards with crayons or colored pens. (If you have access to a camera you could add the students' pictures to the cards. Putting six children in each picture saves film and makes the pictures small enough to fit on the card.) Encourage the students to wear their identification cards while they work on *Choices and Changes.* Provide large safety pins for them to pin the cards to their clothing, or punch a hole in the top of each card, pull a length of yarn through the hole, and tie the yarn around the student's neck. Plastic badge holders also work well.

7. Tell the students that they make decisions about the work they do in school. Ask them to use the "Choice Cards" and the "Choice Can" to keep track of the decisions they make about the work they do. Every time they choose to do an assignment, or choose not to do an assignment, they should put a choice card in the can. Remind them of this as you move from one assignment to another in class.

Assessment

Distribute *Homegram 8* with copies of page 8-3 from the *Student Journal* and ask the students to give the Homegram to their Homework Helpers.

Follow Through

From this point on, whenever it is appropriate to do so, congratulate the children on the work that they have done and explain that they are very good workers.

STUDENT JOURNAL Page 8-1

Work

Some important points to remember about *work* are these:

- Work can be either **physical effort, thinking effort,** or **both.**

- Work is effort by a worker who **produces something** (a good) or **does something** that is **valued** by someone (provides a service).

- Sometimes work is done **for pay and other times not.**

- Work is something **almost everyone does.**

Draw a picture of yourself doing work that makes you feel good about yourself.

Work I Do That Makes Me Feel Good About Myself

This picture shows me _____

This makes me feel good because _____

_____

STUDENT JOURNAL Page 8-2
The Work I Do

My Name: _____

The work I do at school:

_____

_____

_____

_____

_____

The work I do at home:

_____

_____

_____

_____

_____

STUDENT JOURNAL Page 8-3
The Work I Did Today

My Name: _____

Date: _____

The work I did today at school:

_____

_____

_____

_____

_____

_____

The work I did today at home:

_____

_____

_____

_____

_____

_____

WORKER IDENTIFICATION CARDS

Name School Job	Name School Job
Name School Job	Name School Job
Name School Job	Name School Job

HOMEGRAM 8

Dear Homework Helper,

For the next few weeks, students will be learning about the work that they do in school and at home. We are trying to help students understand that they are workers and that the work they do at school and at home is as valuable as anything that adults do. We hope that they will understand how work at school helps them become more powerful individuals. Any encouragement you can give them will be very helpful.

We are helping them keep track of the work they do in school and would appreciate it if you would do the same at home. If your student is not assigned chores at home, it would be helpful if you could speak with him or her about some of the jobs that he or she would like to do. Some suggestions are taking out the garbage, cleaning his or her room, dusting, polishing, sweeping the floors, washing and/or drying the dishes. In addition, it would be helpful to keep track of your student's homework.

I am enclosing five sheets for you to complete each day for the next week with your student. Students should complete the school section in class, but should complete the house-work and homework section with you.

Thank you,

_____

Lesson 9
I Am a Bundle of Human Capital
What can I do?

Cognitive Objectives:

Students will

- Complete a skills inventory.
- Define *human capital* as skills and knowledge.

Affective Objective:

Students will

- Recognize that they have many skills.

Service-learning Objective:

Students will

- Identify the skills they have that will be helpful in doing their service-learning project.

Required Books

- *Those Can Do Pigs* and/or
- Any of the following:
  Amazing Grace
  Aunt Minnie McGranahan
  Big Pumpkin
  The Turnip
  Drylongso

I Like Me
Just the Way You Are
Let Me Do It
Lion Dancer
The Little Engine That Could
Officer Buckle and Gloria
Speak English for Us, Marisol
Tacky the Penguin
Only Passing Through
Rachel's Journal

Required Materials

- A timer
- A passage from a children's book to be typed
- A "Can Do Can" for each student
- Art materials for use in drawing pictures
- *Student Journal,* pages 9-1 and 9-2

Economics Background for Teachers

Human capital is a combination of skills and knowledge. Skills are the things that people can do, and knowledge is the awareness and understanding of facts and relationships.

Vocabulary

- **Alternative:** A possible choice; one of two or more possible actions or choices; opportunities from which people choose.
- **Human capital**: The quality of labor resources which can be improved through investments in education, training, and health; skills and knowledge; also referred to as labor resources.
- **Knowledge**: Awareness and understanding of facts and relationships.
- **Skill**: Something that a person can do.

Preparation

For this lesson the students will observe a typing demonstration that points out the value of human capital (skills and knowledge). To set up the demonstration, arrange to have a computer, a printer, and (if possible) a projector in your classroom, or arrange to take your students to another location suitably equipped for the demonstration.

Contact two people to participate in the demonstration: one should be a skilled keyboarder (such as the school secretary or a parent who uses the computer), the other a person who knows how to type but is not proficient (perhaps another teacher, a parent, or an older student). Explain that each of them will type the same passage from a children's book; the purpose will be to demonstrate how people's human capital differs in different skill areas.

For the demonstration, select a passage from one of the children's books recommended for use with this lesson. Prepare a copy of the passage for each typist. Schedule the day and time for the demonstration.

Getting Started

Tell the students that today they will witness an important contest. They will have to be the judges, so they should pay careful attention. Introduce the two contestants and explain that each of the contestants will perform the same task—typing a page as quickly and with as few errors as possible. Provide a copy of the passage to each contestant.

Ask one of your students to be the timer and to prompt the first typist to begin. When the first typist has finished, the timer should record the time on the board and ask the typist to print a copy of his or her work. Follow the same procedure for the second typist. Then ask each typist to proofread the passage he or she has typed and count the errors. While waiting for the error count, help the students figure out the difference in typing time between the faster and the slower typist. Then compare the number of errors made by the typists.

Ask the students to determine which contestant is the more skilled typist. Consider both time and accuracy.

Have the students discuss why they think one typist is more skilled than the other. *(More training, more practice, more talent for typing.)* Point out that people have varying levels of skills in different areas. Whereas one person might be more skilled at typing than another person, the second person may be more skilled in math or music or dance or economics. Thank the contestants for their demonstration.

Teaching Procedures

1. Read *Those Can Do Pigs*. Have the students list all the things the Can Do Pigs can do. *(Take baths, scrub their snouts, shine their shoes, tie their ties, take a ride, change a tire, fix the fan belt, build roads, mend tables, lamps and chairs, sing, play*

a piano with a stick, beat the bongos with a brick, can-can, row a boat, climb trees, hang by their knees, fly, clean the house, rocket to the moon, ride bulls, build a snow hog, coast down a hill, bake a cake.) Explain that the story is a fable, and the pigs exhibit many human skills.

Write the word "skills" on the board. Explain that skills are things that people (or pigs) can do. The contestants in the typing demonstration displayed their typing skills. A list of the skills the typists possess might include turning the computer on and off, knowing where the letters and numbers are located, pushing down the keys in the right order, moving fingers quickly, typing without looking at the keys, typing without many errors, checking for errors, correcting errors. Both the pigs in the book and the typists have many skills. Do you?

(Optional) Read any of the other books from the **Required Books** list and ask the students to identify the skills possessed by the characters. *(In* Amazing Grace, *Grace can dance and sing, and she has perseverance. In* Big Pumpkin, *and* Officer Buckle and Gloria, *the characters learned to cooperate with others to achieve a goal. In* Aunt Minnie McGranahan, *the children learned to cooperate to get a job done. In* Just the Way You Are, *the characters could carve, paint, sing and play the mandolin, and learn. However, they lacked the skill that the king most valued— caring for others.*
In I Like Me, *the pig exhibits many skills such as drawing, riding bikes, reading, brushing her teeth, keeping clean, eating good food, overcoming obstacles, and working well alone. In* Let Me Do It, *the little girl works hard to learn how to do things. In* Tacky the Penguin, *Tacky has a skill that the other penguins don't know about; he is able to overcome his fear.)* Explain to the students that many people have skills we don't know about or value until they become visible and useful. Explain to them that people don't usually possess all of the skills listed on the board, but it is helpful to learn as many of these as possible. In some of the books, the characters' skills weren't known or appreciated until those skills were helpful to others. (Tacky the Penguin is a good example.) It is important not to judge people who don't appear to have skills or who appear to be different.

2. Ask the students to turn to page 9-1 in their journals; have them develop a list of skills that they possess. Ask them to share the skills they listed with the class. Write the skills they mention on the board. Help them if they are having difficulty listing their skills. The skills might include the ability to read, ride a bike, ride a bus to town, walk to school, make breakfast, follow instructions, listen carefully, learn some economics vocabulary, draw, sing, skateboard, play ball, swim, blow bubble gum, and so on.

3. Write the word "knowledge" on the board. Explain to the students that knowledge is awareness and understanding of facts and relationships. Help them

state some of the things that they know. Depending on the grade, it could be things as simple as their address, phone number, or some much more sophisticated knowledge.

4. If the students' remarks suggest positive attitudes or good work habits (such as being on time) which can't be easily categorized as skills, but could be characterized as qualities or behavior, you can include these attitudes or habits in the skills list, since they help people improve skills and build knowledge. One especially important behavior is cooperation. Students may be surprised to learn that more people are fired from their jobs because they do not get along with other workers than because they cannot do their jobs. Point out that skills of interaction are also important for doing well in school. Have the students name some of the skill and knowledge items from the list that are especially valuable in school. Put a star beside them.

5. Tell the students that you are going to see if they can work cooperatively in teams. Have them form groups of three. Ask them to discuss and then draw pictures of one thing that each member of their group can do. (There should be three pictures per group.) Have them present the results to the class. The pictures will go on a bulletin board. Tell the students that the title of the bulletin board will be Our Human Capital. Write the words "human capital" on the board. Tell the children that human capital is the combination of skills and knowledge that someone possesses.

The bulletin board will consist of the pictures that they have drawn, but they should also bring to school a photograph of them doing the thing that their pictures represent. (If they can't bring in pictures, you may be able to take a picture of them doing the action at school.) Tell the students that they have helped identify some of the skills they possess and that, as you continue with *Choices and Changes*, they will add to this list of skills and knowledge. As the year progresses, you can extend the human capital resources inventory by taking pictures of students as they do their work in school so that it covers a wall from floor to ceiling. This is a great motivator and gives the students a sense of empowerment.

6. Write the words "Hunka Hunka Human Capital" on the board and tell the children that from now on, when they look in the mirror, they should say, "Hello, you hunka hunka human capital."

Assessment

1. Have the children empty their "Choice Cans." Tell them that, from now on, these cans will be "Can Do Cans." For the rest of the year, you will ask the students to place a card in the can every Friday, listing a skill that they worked on that week. Every Monday, they will be asked to explain the card to the class.

2. Review any book you have used in *Choices and Changes* so far. Use Activity 9-1 to make a list of the skills and knowledge possessed by a character in that book. When the students have completed Activity 9-1 as a class, ask them if they think they would like to work with this character. Have them explain why they would or would not want to work with him or her. Have the students turn to page 9-2 in their journals. Have them choose another character and repeat the process you demonstrated for the class.

Follow Through

Each morning when the students come to class, ask them how they have improved their human capital since you last saw them. Every Monday, ask the students to empty their Can Do cans and ask selected students to explain one of their cards. From time to time, address different students as "You hunka hunka human capital."

Some school skills you can suggest to students:
Reads
Writes
Counts, adds, subtracts
Listens
Speaks clearly, using proper grammar
Accepts responsibility, doesn't make excuses
Completes work on time
Uses a computer to accomplish tasks
Cooperates with others to get a job done
Cooperates with others at play
Follows instructions
Perseveres
Teaches
Works well alone

STUDENT JOURNAL Page 9-1

My Human Capital Inventory:
Things I Know and Things I Can Do

My Name _____

Some things I know:

- _____

- _____

- _____

- _____

- _____

- _____

Some things I can do:

- _____

- _____

- _____

- _____

- _____

- _____

STUDENT JOURNAL PAGE 9-2
Human Capital Inventory

Things _____ knows.

_____

_____

_____

_____

_____

Things _____ can do.

_____

_____

_____

_____

_____

ACTIVITY 9-1

Human Capital Inventory

Things _____ knows.

- _____
- _____
- _____
- _____
- _____
- _____

Things _____ can do.

- _____
- _____
- _____
- _____
- _____
- _____

Lesson 10
School Is an Investment in Human Capital

Why am I in school?

Cognitive Objectives:

Students will

- Define *investment in human capital* as developing skills and knowledge.
- Identify schoolwork as an investment in human capital.

Affective Objectives:

Students will

- Recognize that development of human capital increases the quantity and quality of alternatives available to them now and in the future.
- Take responsibility for their education.

Required Books

- *Richard Wright and the Library Card*
- *More Than Anything Else*

Optional Books

Each book illustrates a situation where individuals found ways to invest in their human capital.

- *La Mariposa*
- *Thank You, Mr. Falker*

- *The Bee Tree*
- *Tomas and the Library Lady*
- *Knots on a Counting Rope*
- *Leo the Late Bloomer*
- *Philipok*
- *The Upside Down Boy*

Required Materials

- Activity 10-1

Economics Background for Teachers

Students learn that school is an investment in human capital. Companies invest by buying factories and tools, such as computers, and by increasing their inventories. With investment, businesses give up something that they could do now with their resources, but they do so in order to be more productive in the future. That is precisely the purpose of investment in human capital—to develop skills and knowledge now in order to derive benefits in the future. Students invest in their human capital mainly through their efforts to learn in school (although of course they learn in other ways, too).

Why should students invest in human capital? In order to broaden their range of choices in the future. People who develop ample skills and knowledge in school have more alternatives from which to choose when they leave school. They can choose from a rich array of jobs or opportunities for continuing education because they have skills and knowledge that can be used in many different ways.

Vocabulary

- **Human capital**: The quality of labor resources which can be improved through investments in education, training, and health; skills and knowledge. Also referred to as labor resources.
- **Investment in human capital**: Development of skills and knowledge.
- **Knowledge**: Awareness and understanding of facts and relationships.
- **Skills**: Some things that people can do.

Preparation

Invite two skilled professionals to visit the class. One might be someone who has completed a great deal of schooling; another would be a skilled craftsperson who learned a trade through means other than formal schooling. Tell them that you would like them to tell your students how they acquired their skills and to explain how they use the skills in their work. It is important that they stress both skills that are learned in school and skills learned outside of school. Explain that they will visit the class on the same day; it would be helpful if they could compare notes before making their presentations.

Getting Started

Write the word "investment" on the board. Explain that most people think of investment as saving money in banks, buying land, and acquiring other things that will earn them money. In fact, when businesses build stores and factories and buy new equipment, they are investing.

In a previous lesson the students learned about human capital, skills, and knowledge. Today they will learn about a special kind of investment that every student can make without using any money—that is, investment in human capital. Tell the students that their work in school amounts to an investment in their own human capital. When they develop skills and knowledge through their efforts in school, they invest in their own human capital. School provides the *opportunity* to invest; their *use* of this opportunity, through effort and achievement, clinches the investment—producing human capital that will broaden their range of choices in the future.

Teaching Procedures

1. Read *Richard Wright and the Library Card*. Explain to the class that slaves were not allowed to learn to read in most places in the United States where slavery was permitted. After the Civil War, slaves were freed, but many of the prejudices and restrictions that existed before the War continued afterwards. In the setting described in this book, most of the people didn't want African-Americans to read. Ask the following questions:

- Why did some white people not want African-Americans to learn to read? *(Reading is a skill that allows people to do many new things, and some white people did not want African-Americans to gain new opportunities.)*
- What types of reading enable people to do new things? *(Answers might include reading recipes, directions on packages, instructions on video games, books or magazines to learn about people and places, traffic signs, bus schedules, computer instructions, books in church, and so on.)*

2. Read *More Than Anything Else*. Ask the students why they think Booker was so eager to learn to read. Explain that your job as a teacher is to help the students learn to read so that they can do all of the things that reading enables them to do.

Choices and Changes in Life, School, and Work, © National Council on Economic Education, New York, NY

(Optional) Read *Knots on a Counting Rope*. Ask the following questions:

- What human capital (knowledge and skills) did Boy-Strength-of-Two-Horses lack? *(He could not see; he was blind.)*
- How did the boy learn to see the color blue? *(He felt morning; he heard sunrise in the song of the birds; and he felt the sky when he breathed its softness. He learned that blue is the morning, the sunrise, the sky, the song of the birds, happiness.)*
- How did the boy and his horse learn the trails? *(They traced the trail in their minds. He learned from the horse when to turn by the pull of her neck and by counting her gallops.)*
- What did the boy win when he and his horse finished the race? *(He raced the darkness and he won.)*
- What will happen when the rope is full of counting knots? *(The boy will be able to tell the story himself.)*
- What skills did the boy learn? *(He learned to train his horse to take him to the sheep; he learned to train the horse to race; he learned to touch, feel, hear; and he learned to conquer his fear.)*
- How did this learning affect him? *(He became a more powerful individual because his development of skills and knowledge gave him more alternatives.)*
- How does your learning in school affect you? *(Students will become more powerful individuals because their skills and knowledge will give them more alternatives in life.)*

3. Have the guests discuss their special skills with the students. Ask the students to take notes on the presentations, writing a list of the skills of each speaker, how each speaker acquired those skills, and what investment each speaker made in his or her human capital.

4. Present the students with Activity 10-1 and explain that the list shown there includes some of the skills that will be useful to them now and in the future. Explain any skills on the list that the students may not understand. (An alternative is to show them their report card forms.) Explain that the reason they are in school is to invest in their human capital by developing these skills and others. With the children's help, make a bulletin board listing and perhaps illustrating these skills and put the bulletin board on the wall. Label it "My Human Capital Checklist." Use this bulletin board (or a transparency of Activity 10-1) to help the students when they use their "Can Do Cans" each Friday.

5. Help the students understand that studying is an investment in human capital that increases knowledge. Much like the guest speakers, they have an opportunity to invest in their human capital. Their choices, today and in the future, will affect their human capital positively or negatively, determining the quantity and quality of the alternatives available to them when they leave school.

Assessment

In order for students to take responsibility for their education, they should be able to perform a self-evaluation. Explain that their report cards represent your evaluation of how they are developing their human capital. But they can do a self-assessment. If you deem it appropriate to do so, give the students a blank report card to use for this purpose. Alternatively, you may use the Human Capital Check List provided on Activity 10-1. One advantage of using report cards here is that the activity might tend to demystify the report cards, making them seem a familiar part of the students' educational experience rather than something that "appears" only at specific intervals during the school year. Also, from time to time, ask the students to use their "Can Do Cans" and the Human Capital Checklist from their journals to complete their report cards.

Follow Through

At appropriate times in subsequent classroom activity, prompt the students to remember that school provides them with an opportunity to invest in their human capital. Remind them that more human capital acquired now will provide them with more and better alternatives later in their lives. Human capital is the key to their success. Have students complete a Report Card, a Human Capital Checklist, or a Job Application such as Student Journal 10-1 for characters in any of the books used in *Choices and Changes*.

STUDENT JOURNAL Page 10-1
A Capital Resource

Capital resources are the tools, machines, equipment, and buildings used to produce goods or perform services.

Benefits of capital resources:

—Help produce goods and services <u>faster.</u>

—Can make work <u>easier.</u>

—Help produce <u>better</u> goods and services

A Capital Resource I Would Like to Learn to Use

Find a picture of a machine or tool that you would like to learn how to use. If you can't find a picture in a newspaper or a magazine, you may draw one.

This is a _____ . I would like to

learn to use this capital resource because _____

Activity 10-1
My Human Capital Checklist

Reads

Writes

Counts, adds, subtracts

Listens

Speaks clearly, using proper grammar

Accepts responsibility, doesn't make excuses

Completes work on time

Uses a computer to accomplish tasks

Cooperates with others to get a job done

Cooperates with others at play

Follows instructions

Perseveres

Teaches

Works well alone

This week I have been working on these skills:

_____

_____

_____

_____

The knowledge that I have been gaining this week includes:

_____

_____

_____

_____

UNIT THREE
LEARNING TO PRODUCE

UNIT THREE
Overview: Learning to Produce

The focus of Unit 3 is on using and improving human capital. Children learn to develop a plan to combine their human capital with other resources to produce a product. Through making paper puzzles (or other goods) students discover how practice and teaching others can improve their own human capital, and how to choose among alternatives using those resources.

Lesson 11. Workers Use Other Resources

Students read *The Tortilla Factory, Mike Mulligan and His Steam Shovel,* and *Arthur's Pet Business* to identify additional types of resources. They combine resources to make a holiday product such as a valentine, a snowflake, or a jack-o-lantern. They use their student journals to identify resources around them.

Lesson 12. Inputs, Plan, Outputs

Students read from a list of books that describe cooked or baked products. From the books they learn that production involves inputs, a plan, and outputs. They cook something at home and bring it to school.

Lesson 13. Learning to Produce

Students read *Pink Paper Swans* or another from a list of books to discover that production requires learning. They learn to make a product. This lesson can be used with a multicultural unit.

Lesson 14. Practice

Students read *Sweet Clara and the Freedom Quilt* to discover the importance of practice and other methods for improving their human capital. They practice making the product from lesson 13 and find that practice helps make the product faster, easier, and/or better.

Lesson 15. Teaching Others Builds Human Capital

Students read *Treemonisha* or one from a list of books. They make a list of the skills that a good teacher possesses. They develop a lesson plan to teach a younger student how to produce the good that they have been making in lessons 13 and 14. They teach the lesson and review their teaching experience. They take the lesson home and teach someone in their home.

Lesson 11
Workers Use Other Resources
What can I use to make things?

Cognitive Objectives:

Students will

- Define *resources* as things that people can use to produce goods or services.
- Identify human capital as a resource.
- Identify examples of land.
- Identify examples of physical capital.
- Recognize how capital resources help workers do their jobs faster, easier, and/or better.

Required Books

- *The Tortilla Factory*
- *Mike Mulligan and His Steam Shovel*
- *Arthur's Pet Business*

Optional Books

- *Charlie Needs a Cloak*
- *The Giving Tree*
- *The Trees of the Dancing Goats*
- *Who Uses This?*

Required Materials

- One valentine heart (or another figure suitable to the time of year or your students' ethnic background) made from brightly colored construction paper
- Brightly colored construction paper, two sheets per student
- Scissors, one pair per student
- Old newspaper or magazine with pictures of physical capital.
- Activity 11-1, duplicated to provide one pattern per student (for best results, duplicate the pattern on sturdy paper, such as construction paper or card stock)
- *Student Journal*, pages 7-2, 7-3, 11-1, 11-2

Economics Background for Teachers

Resources are things that people can use to produce goods and services. Four types of resources are human capital (skills and knowledge), land (natural resources), physical capital (goods and services that are produced for the purpose of producing something else), and entrepreneurship (innovation and risk taking). Intermediate goods are products that are used up in the production of goods and services; examples of intermediate goods include flour used in making a cake, paper used in an office, and so on. These resources and intermediate goods are the inputs used to produce a product (or output).

Vocabulary

- **Entrepreneur**: A person who organizes productive resources, takes risks, and finds new ways of combining resources to produce a product.
- **Entrepreneurship**: The ability and willingness to take risks and combine resources in a new way to produce a better product.
- **Human capital**: The quality of labor resources which can be improved through investments in education, training, and health; skills and knowledge; also referred to as labor resources.
- **Land resources**: Gifts of nature; resources that are present without human intervention; also referred to as natural resources.
- **Physical capital**: Goods produced and used to produce other goods and services (capital resources.)
- **Resources**: Things that can be used to produce goods or services.

Preparation

Make a sample valentine heart and collect the materials listed in "Required Materials" above. (In this project alternative objects can be substituted to coincide with the season. Projects for fall might feature a leaf or pumpkin; for winter, a holiday tree or snowflake; for spring, a flower or May basket.)

Getting Started

Write the word "resource" on the board. Explain to the class that they have already learned about one kind of resource—human capital. During the next two days, they will learn about other types of resources. Resources are things that can be used to produce goods and services. Without resources, nothing can be produced. It is because resources are limited that scarcity exists. If we had unlimited resources, we could have everything we want.

Write the words "land," "physical capital," and "entrepreneurship" on the board.

Tell the class that *land* refers to any natural resource. It can refer literally to what the word suggests—farmland, for example. But the concept of land also refers to such things as oil that is used to make gasoline and water that irrigates fields.

Physical capital refers to a good that is produced and used to produce other goods and services. Physical capital includes the tools, machines, equipment, and buildings used to produce goods or perform services. Hammers, computers, rulers, and pencils are all examples of physical capital.

Entrepreneurship refers to a person's ability and willingness to take risks, combining other resources in a new way to produce new products or to produce existing products in a faster or better way.

Have the students repeat the four types of resources: human capital, land, physical capital, and entrepreneurship.

Teaching Procedures

1. Read *Mike Mulligan and His Steam Shovel*. Ask the following questions:

- What type of a resource is the steam shovel? *(Physical capital.)*
- When Mike combined his human capital with Mary Anne's physical capital, what were they able to do? *(They dug canals for boats, passages through mountains for trains, routes for highways, landing fields for airplanes, and deep holes for cellars of tall skyscrapers.)*
- When gasoline shovels replaced steam shovels, what did Mike Mulligan and Mary Anne do? *(Mary Anne became the furnace for the new town hall, and Mike became the janitor.)*

2. Read *Arthur's Pet Business*. Ask the following questions:

- Which type of resource does Arthur demonstrate? *(Entrepreneurship.)*
- How did Arthur plan to show his parents that he could be responsible for a pet? *(He would take care of other people's pets.)*

- How did Arthur and Francine let people know that he was in business? *(They advertised by putting up signs.)*
- What kind of dog was Perky supposed to be—friendly or mean? *(Mean.)*
- How did Arthur take care of Perky? *(He brushed her, fed her her favorite foods, and walked her.)*
- What happened as word of Arthur's business spread? *(The business grew.)*
- Why had Perky been so mean? *(She was having babies.)*
- Did Arthur do a good job taking care of the pets? What are the advantages of running your own business and what are the disadvantages? Do you think running your own business is better than working for someone? *(Accept various answers. Tell the students that they will learn more about entrepreneurs in a later class.)*

3. Read *The Tortilla Factory*.

- Before reading tell the students that as you read the story, they should identify resources mentioned in the story. Divide the class into pairs for this task; tell them that the pair with the most correct answers will have a special job later in the class.
- After reading ask which types of resources the story mentions. *(The resources are as follows: black earth–land; brown hands–human capital; yellow seeds–land; tortilla factory–physical capital; laughing people–human capital; clank-clunking machinery–physical capital; truck–physical capital.)*

4. Ask the students to discover resources around their home and school. Have them use page 11-1 in their journals to record the resources they discover. In the first column they should name the resource; in the second column they should identify the resource type (human capital, land, physical capital, or entrepreneurship).

5. Ask the students to make two valentines (or pumpkins or any other holiday item). Show the class a valentine heart you have made from construction paper. Give each student a piece of construction paper and direct each to make a valentine heart like the one you made. Tell them there are special rules for this activity: they can use only their hands, they must stand, and they cannot place the paper on their desks while working on the hearts. Challenge them to make their valentines look as much like yours as they can. Encourage neatness, but emphasize that they should work as quickly as possible. Note how long it takes most of them to complete the task.

6. When the students have finished, ask what might help them make their hearts look more like your sample. They will probably suggest using scissors and pencils; they may also mention a pattern. To follow up on this discussion, give each student more construction paper, Activity 11-1 (the pattern), scissors, and a pencil. Talk with the students about how they might use these tools to make improved

versions of their valentine hearts. If any students need help, show them how to use the pencil to draw around the pattern on the construction paper, and how to use the scissors to cut out the hearts. Also, allow them to work seated at their desks this time. Again, encourage neatness and working quickly. Note how long it takes most students to complete the task.

7. When the students have completed these second efforts, ask the following questions:

- Which valentine looks more like the example I showed you—the first or the second? *(For all or most students, the second.)*
- What physical capital helped you make the second heart? *(scissors, pencils, pattern, desks.)*
- Which heart was easier to make? *(The second.)* Ask someone who answers, "the second," why it was easier. *(They were able to use physical capital.)*
- Which valentine did you make faster? *(For most students the second will have been faster. Provide them with a comparison of the times.)* Ask someone who made the second heart more quickly why it was faster. *(Able to sit at desk, to use pattern, pencil, and scissors.)*
- To review the activity, ask "What were the advantages of using the pencil, pattern, scissors, and desk?" *(Using tools helped make the second valentine better and neater in appearance; tools also enabled students to work faster and to do the work more easily.)* Emphasize the point that students use physical capital every day to do their work.

8. Help the students recall the meanings of *goods* and *services*. Ask them whether they were making a good or performing a service when they made their valentines. *(Making a good.)*

9. Ask students to name the physical capital they used. *(Pencil, pattern, scissors, and desk.)* Refer to the definition provided earlier.

NOTE: If anyone names the construction paper as a capital resource, explain that paper is not a capital resource in this case because it is used up in the process of making the valentine. Capital resources do not get used up when you produce a good, at least not immediately. They are used to help produce more than one good or service. The construction paper is an intermediate good.

10. Tell the students that most workers use physical capital to help them do their work. Distribute the *Student Journals* and have the students look again at the workers depicted on pages 7-2 and 7-3. Review the pictures and ask the students to identify the physical capital these workers probably use. For example, a carpenter uses a saw, a barber uses a razor, and a mail carrier uses a sack. If you used *"Who Uses This?"* in Lesson 7, you can refer to it here.

11. Discuss the difficulty some workers would have in trying to produce their goods or perform their services without specific capital resources. Most workers in fast food restaurants, for example, depend on one or more capital resources in their jobs. Food preparers use knives, spatulas, and mixers; cooks use grills, fryers, and ovens; servers use ice makers, drink dispensers, and ice cream machines; cashiers use cash registers; dishwashers use dishwashing machines.

12. Write on the chalkboard:
   Benefits of Capital Resources:
   • Help produce goods and services **faster**
   • Make work **easier**
   • Help produce **better** goods and services

13. Review these three points, mentioning some familiar ways in which physical capital helps specific workers do their work faster, easier, and/or better. For example, grocery clerks can check out customers faster and probably more accurately by using cash registers or electronic scanners. Discuss how other workers depicted in the journals benefit from the capital resources they use.

Assessment

1. Turn students' attention to page 11-1 in their journals and review the definition of resources. Have them turn to page 11-2 in their *Student Journal.* Ask them to use a newspaper or magazine to find a tool or piece of equipment *(physical capital)* that they would like to learn to use. When they have finished, ask them to explain how the capital resource would help them make a good or perform a service. *(Examples of capital resources in which students might be interested are computers, construction equipment, airplanes, stage equipment, or a stove or oven.)*

2. Have the students complete a report card (Activity 3.1) or a human capital checklist (Activity 10.1) for Arthur. Have them write a job application form for Arthur's dog-sitting job. In this job application, they should use the human capital checklist (Activity 10.1) to describe the skills and knowledge a person working as a pet sitter should have.

Follow Through

As the students discover examples of resources in the classroom, you can label the examples with signs—e.g, computer = physical capital, classroom = physical capital, teacher = human capital, school grounds = land. From time to time, have the children write job application forms for different jobs.

STUDENT JOURNAL Page 11-1
Resources I Have Discovered

Name of the Resource	Type of Resource

Activity 11-1
Valentine Heart Pattern

Activity 11-2
Job Application

Uncle Jed's Barbershop

Name _____ Date of Birth _____

Address_____ Phone Number _____

Position for which you are applying: <u>Barbershop helper</u>

Education and training _____

_____

_____

Work experience _____

_____

_____

Special skills you possess _____

_____

_____

Why should Uncle Jed hire you? _____

_____

_____

_____

References:

Name: _____ Relationship _____

Address: _____ Phone number _____

Name: _____ Relationship _____

Address: _____ Phone number _____

Lesson 12

Inputs, Plan, Outputs

Can I actually produce something?

Cognitive Objectives:

Students will

- Define *production* as using resources to produce a good or service.
- Define *intermediate goods* as things that are used up in the production process.
- Define *inputs* as resources and intermediate goods.
- Define *production plan* as a method for producing a good or service.
- Define *outputs* as products or goods or services.

Affective Objective:

Students will

- Take pride in their ability to produce something.

Service-learning Objectives:

Using the decision-making apron, students will

- Decide if they want to produce a good for someone or some group.
- [If so] decide what to produce and how to produce it.

Required Books

Any of the following:

- *Bruno the Baker*
- *Cook-a-Doodle-Doo* and *The Little Red Hen*
- *How to Make an Apple Pie* and *See the World*
- *Jalapeno Bagels*
- *Saturday Sancocho*
- *The Ugly Vegetables*

Optional Books

- *Chato's Kitchen*
- *The House I'll Build for the Wrens*
- *The Goat in the Rug*

Required Materials

- *Student Journal*, pages 7-1, 12-1
- A recipe of your own choosing
- Homegram 12

Economics Background for Teachers

In this lesson, children learn about production. Production is the use of resources to make goods or perform services. As students have already learned, goods are *things* and services are *actions*. In order to produce a good, the producer must use different kinds of inputs, including human capital and other resources, as well as intermediate goods. Intermediate goods are goods that are used up in the act of production; intermediate goods include, for example, the construction paper used in Lesson 11 or flour used in baking. The producer must develop a production plan to combine resources and intermediate goods to produce the product. "Output" is simply another word for product. Production is a process in which people use a plan to combine inputs to produce an output.

Vocabulary

- **Intermediate goods:** Products that are used up in the production of goods and services.
- **Inputs:** Resources and intermediate goods.
- **Output**: A product (good or service).
- **Production**: Using resources to produce a good or service.
- **Production plan:** A method for producing a good or service.

Getting Started

Tell the students that they have already begun to learn about goods and services. In this lesson they are going to learn about production of goods and services. Review the meaning of *goods* and *services* briefly. Then explain the vocabulary terms, emphasizing the point that the process of production requires inputs and a plan.

To introduce the relationships among these concepts, write the following on the board:

Inputs (resources and intermediate goods) + Production plan = Output (goods and services)

Then take the students back to page 7-1 in their journals, where they have previously identified different goods and services. Explain that they were producing an item when they made the valentines (or other items) in Lesson 11. They used resources and they combined them in order to produce a product.

Teaching Procedures

1. Read *Bruno the Baker* or *Cook-a-Doodle-Doo* and *The Little Red Hen* or *How to Make an Apple Pie* and *See the World* or *Jalapeno Bagels* or *Saturday Sancocho* or *The Ugly Vegetables*. If you use *Cook-a-Doodle-Doo*, you may want to read *The Little Red Hen* first and have the students compare the experiences of the little red hen to those of Cook-a-Doodle-Doo.

- Explain that the characters in each story used different inputs, had a production plan, and produced an output.
- Ask the students to identify the inputs that were used. *(The inputs would include the human [or animal] capital, the intermediate goods [ingredients for the product], physical capital [measuring instruments, pots and pans, stove or oven]. Each book provides a recipe at the end of the story, so the inputs are easy to identify.)*
- Ask students to identify the production plan. *(The recipe.)*

2. Ask the students what other products are made in an economy. *(While the list may include food items, be sure that the students also include other goods and services such as computers, automobiles, bicycles, and video games. Explain that, in producing all of these goods, producers use a "recipe" that includes the resources to be used in production and the methods of production. This recipe is called a production plan. Review the fact that a production plan is a method for producing a good or service that is thought about before beginning production.)*

3. (**Optional**) You can use *Chato's Kitchen* to help the students see what is involved in planning a party.

4. The students now know enough about resources and production to begin production of their service-learning project, whether it is a good or a service. Once they decide what the output will be, help them identify the resources that will be used and the production plan. What activities will be done, who will be contacted, who will gather the resources, who will do the producing? Will the class want to ask some adults to lend their human capital to the process? Once the production plan is developed, help the students assign tasks to individuals and set deadlines for each stage of the project.

Assessment

1. Have the students make one of the products from the books or any other baked or cooked item at home. Arrange for adults to help with the cooking, but be sure that the students do the actual production. Make copies of page 12-1 of their *Student Journal* and have them take those home with Homegram 12. Include a recipe from one of the books or one that you would like each student to prepare. You can vary the recipes so that different students bring in different baked goods. Have them bring in their products for a party for students in another grade or for a visit to a homeless shelter or some other group.

2. Have the students do a "Human Capital Checklist" or a report card for any of the characters in the book you have used for this lesson. Have them write a job application for a cook. In this job application, they should list the human capital that will be required for a cook.

Follow Through

You can return to this lesson for your service-learning project.

Homegram

Distribute *Homegram 12* and ask the children to take it home and give it to their Homework Helper.

STUDENT JOURNAL Page 12-1
Inputs, Plan, Output

My Name _____

I produced a _____

The resources I used were: _____

_____

_____

_____

The intermediate goods (ingredients) I used were: _____

_____

_____

_____

This is my production plan (recipe): _____

_____

_____

_____

_____

HOMEGRAM 12

Dear Homework Helper,

In class today, the students learned about production. They discovered that production involves resources, intermediate inputs, and a production plan.

In connection with this lesson, their homework is to cook or bake a product at home and to bring it to class on _____ . I would appreciate your help on this assignment. The attached handout may help to organize the production.

Students will use themselves (human capital), some physical capital (pots, pans, measuring cups and spoons, the stove or oven), some intermediate goods (the ingredients in the recipe), and a production plan (the recipe). You are welcome to use the recipe provided below for a(n) _____ _____ or any baked good that you prefer. If you use something different than the _____ please be sure your student includes the recipe on the attached sheet.

Thanks so much for your help.

_____

Choices and Changes in Life, School, and Work, © National Council on Economic Education, New York, NY

Lesson 13
Learning to Produce
Can you learn to produce outputs?

Cognitive Objective:

Students will

• Combine their skills and knowledge with other resources to produce a good.

Affective Objective:

Students will

• Increase their self-confidence by discovering their ability to learn skills.

NOTE: Students will be making a product, one identified in one of the books you select or a Paper Puzzle or a Treasure Box or a Hexaflexagon. Instructions for these items are given at the end of this lesson. Students will continue to make these products in Lesson 14 and Lesson 15.

Required Book

• *Pink Paper Swans.* Directions for making paper swans are included in the book. If your students make this product, they will not need anything other than the paper.

Optional Books

• *Dream Catchers*
• *Making Magic Windows*
• *Magic Windows*

Required Materials

- The materials in the book you select or the materials below:
  - ➢ Rulers (one per student)
  - ➢ Scissors (one pair per student)
  - ➢ *Student Journal*, page 13 - 1
  - ➢ Crayons or colored markers (optional)

Optional Materials

- ➢ Stopwatch
- For Option A: Paper Puzzle
  - ➢ A six-inch square of paper (one square per student)
- For Option B: Treasure Box
  - ➢ A six-inch square of paper (one square per student)
- For Option C: Hexaflexagon
  - ➢ Activity 4, Pattern for Hexaflexagon
  - ➢ Sheets of sturdy 8½″ × 11″ paper (one per student)
  - ➢ Glue or stapler

Economics Background for Teachers

Human capital can be used to produce goods and services. Through learning, increasing their human capital, people can produce new goods and services.

Vocabulary

- **Creativity**: The use of imagination to make something new or different.
- **Improve:** To make better.

Preparation

Decide (or use the decision-making process to help your students decide) which of the products your class will make. Once the decision is made, gather materials and make several of the products yourself so that you can provide oral directions and can demonstrate how to make the product with ease.

Getting Started

Ask the children what new things they have learned to do lately. Some answers might include learning a new skill on the computer, to play a new video game or sport, to ride a bike, play a musical instrument, dance, skate, and so on. Ask the students if the skill was hard to learn at first. Tell them that today they are going to learn to do something that might seem difficult at first. Show them a sample of the product you (or they) have chosen to produce and tell them that they are all going to learn to produce one of these. (Be sure that you have practiced making the product yourself so that it is easy for you to do.)

Teaching Procedures

1. Read *Pink Paper Swans.*

- Write the word "Origami" on the board. Ask the students if they know what the word means. Explain that it refers to a Japanese art form by means of which people make products from paper.
- Ask the students the following questions.
  ➤ Why did Mrs. Tsujimoto make origami products? *(She enjoyed it and she earned some money from selling her products.)*
  ➤ Why did she stop doing origami? *(Her arthritis made it too painful.)*
  ➤ What skill from the students' My Human Capital Checklist (Activity 10-1) did Janetta possess? *(She was able to work well with others.)*
- Explain that Janetta and Mrs. Tsujimoto were able to cooperate to get a job done that neither of them could do alone. Ask the students if Janetta had always known how to do origami. (*No, she had not.*) Explain that Janetta was able to learn how to make pink paper swans and other products just as they are going to learn how to make a product today.

2. Follow one set of directions for making a product below—Option A, B, or C— or follow directions from one of the books mentioned.

3. Have the students identify the skills they used to produce their product. Follow the directions below or make up a similar list for the products your students made from one of the books

4. Distribute the *Student Journals* and ask the students to turn to page 13-1. As a class, work through the questions as students record their answers. What is the name of the good you made? *(Paper puzzle, treasure box, hexaflexagon, or other.)* What human resources (skills and knowledge) did you have before you started? *(Answers will vary depending on the ability levels of the students. Most will have cutting and folding skills. Some will have knowledge of measurement and skills in following directions.)* What new human resources did you need to make the product? *(Answers will depend on students' previous experiences. Some may not*

have needed new human resources.) What was the easiest part of making the product? *(Answers will vary.)* What was the most difficult part of making the product? *(Answers will vary.)*

5. Tell the students that they can now improve their products. Write on the chalkboard:

Improve: To make better.

6. Explain that to improve their products the students might use their creativity. On the chalkboard write:

Creativity is the use of imagination to make something new or different.

You can use creativity to create or improve goods and services. Creativity allows people to think about something in a new or different way. People who sell goods and services use their creativity to make their products as attractive as possible so that more people will want them. Suggest that students use their creativity to color their products or to add "sparkles" or other decorative items.

7. Designers and artists make their living using creativity. For example, some artists use their creativity to design company symbols (logos) that help customers remember the companies' products. Invite the students to suggest creative company symbols (such as McDonald's golden arches and Apple Computer's apple).

8. Have the students complete the last statement on page 13-1 of their journals.

9. Tell the students that you want them to save their first product and that they will be able to make other products later. Have them write their initials and a small "1" somewhere on the product.

Assessment

1. Ask each student to think of one school activity that requires two or more kinds of human resources. One example is doing addition problems; it requires a knowledge of numbers, a knowledge of addition rules, and the skill of writing. On a separate piece of paper, have each student write the name of the activity he or she thinks of and list the human resource (skills and/or knowledge) the activity requires.

2. Ask the students to think about what human resources they used to make their product. Review the steps, writing them on the chalkboard, and then identify the

skill or knowledge that enables the students to carry out each step. Sample answers are provided below.

- Option A: Paper Puzzle
  ➤ Step 1. Cut out a square. (Skill of cutting; skill of measuring; knowledge of shapes.)
  ➤ Step 2. Fold in half both ways. (Skill of folding.)
  ➤ Step 3. Fold four corners to middle. (Skill of folding.)
  ➤ Step 4. Flip and fold corners to middle. (Skill with fingers; skill of folding.)
  ➤ Step 5. Place fingers in pockets and squeeze. (Skill with fingers.)
  ➤ Step 6. Write numbers inside triangles. (Skill of following directions; skill of writing numbers.)

Have the students count the different skills and knowledge they used in making the puzzle.

- Option B: Treasure Box
  ➤ Step 1. Cut out a square. (Skill of cutting; skill of measuring; knowledge of shapes.)
  ➤ Step 2. Fold in half both ways. (Skill of folding.)
  ➤ Step 3. Fold four corners to middle. (Skill of folding.)
  ➤ Step 4. Flip and fold corners to middle. (Skill with fingers; skill of folding.)
  ➤ Step 5. Fold out point of each triangle. (Skill of folding.)
  ➤ Step 6. Flip and fold out point of each square. (Skill with fingers; skill of folding.)

Have students count the different skills and knowledge they used in making the treasure box.

- Option C: Hexaflexagon
  ➤ Step 1. Cut out a paper strip. (Skill of cutting; skill of measuring.)
  ➤ Step 2. Using the triangle pattern, trace 10 triangles on the strip. (Skill of tracing.)
  ➤ Step 3. Score and crease the lines. (Skill of folding.)
  ➤ Step 4. Fold into a shape with six sides. (Skill of folding.)
  ➤ Step 5. Glue. (Skill with fingers.)
  ➤ Step 6. Color. (Art skill.)

Have the students count the different skills and knowledge they used in making the hexaflexagon.

Directions for Options A, B, and C:

(Note: Whichever option you choose, time the **Getting Started** portion of the lesson for use in the next lesson.)

Option A—Paper Puzzle

1. Tell students that today they will make a paper puzzle that they can open and close with their fingers to create number problems.

2. Show them the model you prepared. Tell them that to make it you had to use your human resources—both skills and knowledge—and they will use theirs also to make their own paper puzzles.

3. Distribute the materials to each student. Tell them to listen carefully to the instructions:

- **Step 1** Cut a 6-inch square from your paper.
- **Step 2** Fold the square in half one-way, crease, and unfold. Fold it in half the other way, crease, and unfold. (Broken lines on the illustration show the fold lines.)

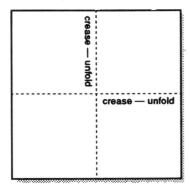

- **Step 3** Fold the four corners of the square to the middle.

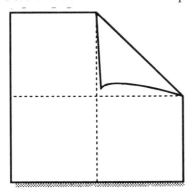

- **Step 4** Turn the square (now 4¼″ × 4¼″) over, placing the folds down on the table. Fold all four corners again to meet in the middle.

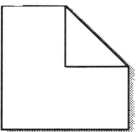

- **Step 5** Fold the form in half one way, crease, and unfold. Fold the form in half the other way, crease, and unfold. Fold the form in half so that the triangle shapes are on the inside and the square shapes are on the outside.

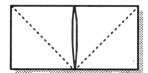

- **Step 6** Stick your thumb and first finger of your right hand into the "pockets" created by the <u>squares </u>on the right side of the form. Stick your left thumb and first finger into the "pockets" on the left side of the form.

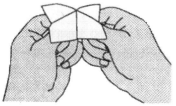

- **Step 7** Squeeze your thumb and finger of each hand together at the bottom of the form. Push your fingers together to open up the center of the form and cause the squares to make "petals."

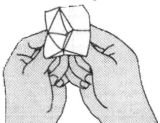

- **Step 8** Push the sides back toward the middle. <u>Let your fingers relax, stop squeezing your thumb and fingers</u> and move them away from each other. Watch the center of the form open the other way.

- **Step 9** Show students how they can write numbers on the inside triangles and practice adding and subtracting by giving answers to number problems that emerge when the "puzzle" is opened in different directions. Or have students make "Fortune-Telling Machines" by writing "fortunes" on the inside of the pockets.

Option B–Treasure Box

1. Tell students that today they will use their human resources to create a good—a small open box in which to display something of value to them.

2. Show them the model you prepared. Tell them that to make it you had to use your human resources—both skills and knowledge—and they will use theirs also to make their own treasure boxes.

3. Distribute the materials and ask them to listen carefully to the instructions: NOTE: Directions for the first five steps are the same as those for making the paper puzzle.

- **Step 1** Cut a 6-inch square from your paper.
- **Step 2** Fold the square in half one-way, crease, and unfold. Fold it in half the other way, crease, and unfold. (Broken lines on the illustration show the fold lines.)

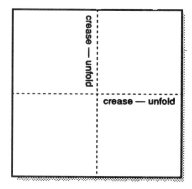

- **Step 3** Fold the four corners of the square to the middle.

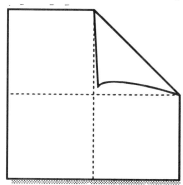

- **Step 4** Turn the square (now 4¼″ × 4¼″) over, placing the folds down on the table. Fold all four corners again to meet in the middle.

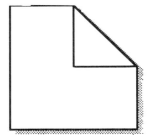

- **Step 5** Fold the form in half one way, crease, and unfold. Fold the form in half the other way, crease, and unfold. Fold the form in half so that the triangle shapes are on the inside and the square shapes are on the outside.

- **Step 6** Place the form on the table with the squares down and the triangles pointing up. Fold the point of each triangle out to meet the outside edge of the form.

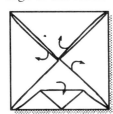

- **Step 7** Turn the form over so the squares are up. (Your form should look like a square "table" resting on triangular "legs.") Fold the inner corner of each square back about one-half inch.

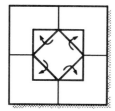

- **Step 8** Stick the first finger of one hand inside the corner created by one of the points you folded back. Open up the corner with your finger. With the thumb and first finger of your other hand, pinch the sides of the corner on the outside of the square to help hold the square open.

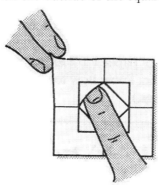

- **Step 9** Follow the same procedure for the three other corners. All four corners should now be open and should form an open "box." The triangles on the underside of the form will create a base for the box.

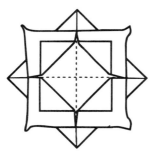

Option C—Hexaflexagon

1. Tell students that today they are going to use their human resources to create a good. The name of the good they will make is a word that is fun to say—*hexaflexagon* (hek - se - flek'-se - gön). Have students repeat the name a few times to see how fast they can say it. Explain that "hex" means "six." Explain that a hexaflexagon is a hand puzzle that flips and twists. They can play with it by themselves or invent games with it to play with another person.

2. Show students the hexaflexagon model you prepared. Tell them that to make the model you had to use your human resources—both skills and knowledge. They will have to use their human resources to make their hexaflexagons.

3. Distribute to each student the paper for a hexaflexagon, Activity 4, *Patterns for Hexaflexagon,* a ruler, and a pencil (if they do not have one). Tell students to listen carefully as you give the following directions.

- **Step 1** Measure a strip of paper 1½ inches wide and 11 inches long. (If students do not know how to use a ruler, demonstrate how to read the markings.)
- **Step 2** Cut out the strip.
- **Step 3** Place the strip so that the longest part goes from left to right (not up and down). Put your triangle at the left side of the strip with the 'T' point at the top of the paper. Line up the base of your triangle with the bottom of the strip. Trace the outline of the triangle onto the paper. When you have created the first triangle, turn your pattern over to create a second triangle beside it. Your first triangle will be right side up, the second upside down, and so on. (See the illustration below; you may need to draw the illustration on the chalkboard.) Make 10 triangles. Draw the triangles lightly with your pencil so you can erase them if you need to.

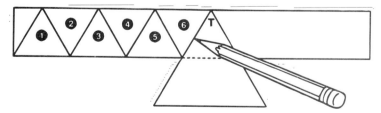

- **Step 4** When your triangles are correct, retrace them with your pencil. This time press hard to score (that is, make a crease in) the paper so the lines will easier to fold.
- **Step 5** Cut off the excess paper at both ends so your strip begins and ends with slanted triangle lines.
- **Step 6** Fold the 10 triangles on the strip back and forth on the scored lines to crease the lines, placing the first triangle up, the second down, and so on. You will end up with the triangles "stacked" on top of each other. (Show students how to fold the triangles following this illustration.)

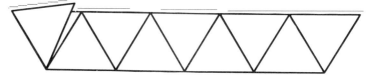

- **Step 7** Flatten out the strip. Lightly number the lines starting with 1 and ending with 11.

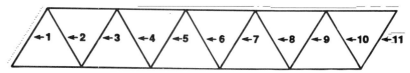

- **Step 8** Now you are ready to fold a hexaflexagon. Hold the strip with your left hand. Fold line 3 to the inside (toward your right hand). Fold line 6 to the inside (toward you). Fold line 9 toward the "1" Side. The folded piece will have six sides.

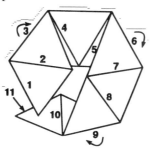

- **Step 9** Glue together the two ends that meet, placing the first triangle over the last triangle. Flatten.

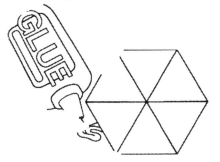

- **Step 10** When the glue is dry, try gently twisting your hexaflexagon on the folds until it flattens out with different sides showing.

NOTE: Larger hexaflexagons can be made if students have access to larger paper. For example, with legal-size paper the size of the hexaflexagon can be increased to 14 inches long by 2 inches wide. Use the same triangle pattern to create 10 larger triangles.

STUDENT JOURNAL Page 13-1
Using My Human Capital to Make a Good

My name is _____

The good I made was a _____

To make my good, I used some skills and knowledge I already had.

Some of the skills and knowledge I used were these:

_____

_____

_____

I did not have some of the human capital I needed to make my good or service. Some of the skills I learned were these:

_____

_____

_____

The easiest part of making the good was _____

The hardest part of making the good was _____

I improved my good by:

_____

_____

_____

It took me _____ minutes to make the good.

Lesson 14
Practice

How can I improve my human capital?

Cognitive Objectives:

Students will

- Recognize that skills can be improved with practice.
- Identify ways to improve human capital.
- Identify ways in which skill improvement leads to the work being done faster, easier, and/or better, so that the product is improved.

Affective Objective:

Students will

- Become accustomed to practice as part of the learning process.

Required Book

- *Sweet Clara and the Freedom Quilt*

Optional Books

- *Amazing Grace*
- *Drawing Lessons from a Bear*
- *Let Me Do It*
- *Eight Hands Round*
- *The Keeping Quilt*
- *The Patchwork Quilt*

Required Materials

- Stopwatch (or watch with a second hand)
- Enough materials for each student to make three of the same product they made in Lesson 13
- Ruler
- Scissors
- Crayons or colored markers
- For Option C, hexaflexagon patterns
- *Student Journal*, page 14-1

Economics Background for Teachers

Practice is one way of investing in human capital.

Vocabulary

- **Practice:** To do something many times for the purpose of learning.

Getting Started

Write the word "practice" on the board. Explain to the students that practice is doing something many times for the purpose of learning. Ask them if they have practiced anything in order to learn. Some examples might be writing their letters, riding a bike, learning a sport, and so on. Explain that they are going to practice making their products.

Teaching Procedures

1. Read *Sweet Clara and the Freedom Quilt*. Ask the students the following questions.

- Why was Aunt Rachel worried about Clara? *(She was not very strong and might not survive in the fields.)*
- Why did Aunt Rachel want Clara to learn to sew? *(Sewing would be a skill that would enable Clara to work inside the Big House. The work inside would be easier, and Clara would have a better chance of surviving.)*
- Why did Aunt Rachel have Clara rip out her work and do it again? *(She knew that more practice would make it more likely that Clara would be allowed to sew for Missus.)*
- How did Clara react to having to make the stitches so tiny? *(She didn't like it.)* Why did she have to make the stitches so tiny? *(She would have to be very skilled to work for Missus.)*

- What choices did Clara make? *(To practice, so that she could improve her human capital; to make the freedom quilt; to run away to freedom; to leave the quilt behind so that others could use it.)*
- What changes did these choices make in Clara's life and the lives of others? *(Clara was able to leave the very hard work in the fields. She gained her freedom. Others were able to gain their freedom.)*
- How did her skill make Clara more powerful? *(She was able to use it to gain her freedom.)*

2. If you read *Amazing Grace*, ask the students why Grace knew exactly what to do when it came her turn to be Peter Pan. *(She had practiced all weekend.)*

3. Remind the students of the previous day's activity which involved using their human capital. Recall with them that they used some knowledge and skills they already had, but they also increased their human capital.

4. Tell the students that today they are going to learn how to improve their human capital through practice.

5. Explain that repeating something improves our work in several ways. Practice improves our skills (just as Clara improved her skills) and it often helps us do our work *faster*. (If we work *too* fast, however, the results of our work may not be as good as when we work more slowly.)

6. If you use *The Patchwork Quilt*, ask the students how long Tanya thought it would take to finish the quilt and how long Grandma said it would take. *(Tanya, no time; Grandma, a year.)*

7. Practice also helps make our work *easier*. As we become more skilled in doing a task, the work seems less difficult.

8. Finally, practice improves our skills and can make our work *better*. With the improvements brought about by practice, the goods or services we produce become neater, more attractive, and may last longer.

9. Explain that there are other ways to improve human capital. Write the following expressions on the board:

> Watch others
> Listen to others
> Read
> Ask questions
> Follow written directions

Explain that these expressions refer to other ways to improve human capital.

10. Tell the students that today they are going to learn to improve their human capital through practice. Refer to the word "Practice" on the board and explain again that practice means doing something many times in order to learn. Explain that repeating something improves our work in several ways. Underneath the word "Practice," write the words "faster," "better," and "easier." Distribute the necessary materials to make the same product they made in the previous lesson.

11. Distribute the *Student Journals* and have the students turn to page 14-1. On this page they will record the results of their practice. Have them repeat the production process from the previous lesson, keeping track of the amount of time it takes to make the product. Have them record the time it took to make the first product, how the product looked and worked, and how hard it was to make. As they practice making the product, they should think about the improvement (or lack of improvement) they see in how their product looks or works and the improvement (or lack of it) in the ease with which they make the product.

12. Explain that for today's practice you will again give the students directions. However, you will go through the directions more quickly than you did before. Direct the students to construct a practice object. If they are able to compute their work time in minutes, have them note starting and finishing times next to "second practice." Otherwise, have everyone start at the same time, and call the time in intervals of half–minutes. Students should use the time you announce that is closest to their actual finishing time.

13. Have the students write their initials and a small "2" somewhere on their object to identify it as their second practice product; they should also record the time in their journals. (They will complete the other columns later.) Answer any questions students may still have about making additional objects.

14. Tell the students they are to make another product without your help (unless you think they still need directions). Emphasize that they are to follow the same steps they have just gone through. Encourage the students to work without your help, but remain available for their questions. Note the starting time as students begin working independently. Time them, or have the students raise their hands when they are finished, and tell them their individual completion times. Have them record their times on page 14-1 of their journals (next to third practice). Have the students initial and put a small "3" somewhere on their product. Then have them go through one or two more practice sessions, depending on available time and student motivation.

15. When the students have completed their practice products, have volunteers report their time results. Did the time they needed to make the products decrease

with more practice? If they answer yes, ask why. *(Faster at measuring, faster at folding, etc.)* If they answer no, ask why. *(Still don't understand, am not a fast folder, etc.)* Discuss whether additional practice might cut down the amount of time needed.

16. Direct the students to place the practice objects they made on their desks, using the numbers they wrote on them to put them in order. Tell them to look carefully at how the objects look and work. How would they rate the one numbered "1"? *(Suggest descriptions such as bad, pretty good, good, very good.)* Have the students rate each of their products (using the second column on page 14-1 of their journals).

17. Ask volunteers to report their assessments of how their products look and work. Did their products get better with practice? If so, it is probably because their human capital has improved. Were any of their later products worse than their first ones? If so, why?

18. Turn the students' attention to the third column on page 14-1 of their journals. This column asks them to think about how easy or difficult it was to make each product. (Suggest descriptions such as very hard, hard, easy, very easy.) Did the products get easier to make with practice? Why? If students do not think the work got easier, why not? Have them write a word or two in their journals to describe the difficulty of making each one.

19. Tell the students that practice is one way to improve our human capital. The time we spend practicing is an investment in ourselves because we are building our resources. Ask the students if they can think of any other ways to improve their human capital. Prompt their thinking by referring to the ways that you listed on the board.

20. Emphasize that people continue to build their human capital throughout their lives. Practicing, watching, listening, reading words, and studying illustrations are all good ways to improve skills and gain knowledge.

Assessment

1. Have the students work in small groups to think of specific ways in which they have improved their human capital through practicing, watching, listening, reading, and asking questions. Have the groups act out the ways they identify. Let remaining class members try to guess what is enacted and how human capital has improved in the situations. Examples might be reading, doing math, tying special knots, drawing, jumping rope, or playing a musical instrument.

2. Have the students complete a report card (Activity 3-1) or a Human Capital Checklist (Activity 10-1) for Sweet Sarah or Grace.

Optional Activity

Review the information about quilting in Lesson 6. Read *Eight Hands Round, The Keeping Quilt,* and *The Patchwork Quilt.* Ask the students if they would like to make a quilt for their service-learning project. A quilt can be made either with cloth or with paper. Ask the students if they would like to make a quilt based on *Eight Hands Round.* Suggest that they could make the quilt and give it to students in a lower grade who could use it to help them learn their alphabet letters. Suggest that they might want to use the patterns in *Eight Hands Round* with the patterns and letters for each pattern on the patches. This is one alternative for their service-learning project. Once the quilt is complete, each student in the class could teach one letter and explain the pattern to students in the lower grade.

STUDENT JOURNAL Page 14-1
Practice Improves My Human Capital

Practice improves our human capital by making our work faster or easier or by making our product better. Sometimes our work gets faster and easier and better with practice.

The product I made is a _____

	Total Minutes	**How my products looked and worked**	**How hard it was to make my products**
1st Practice			
2nd Practice			
3rd Practice			
4th Practice			

Lesson 15
Teaching Others Builds Human Capital
What does it take to be a teacher?

Cognitive Objectives:

Students will

- Recognize that one person can help another improve human capital by teaching him or her new skills or knowledge.
- Describe how teaching also helps build the teacher's human capital by adding to his or her knowledge of the subject and improving organizational and communication skills.
- Develop a plan to teach the necessary steps in a specific skill.
- Identify skills used in teaching as human capital.

Affective Objectives:

Students will

- See the power that a teacher has to help others.
- Connect teaching and learning.

Required Book

- *Treemonisha*

Optional Books

- *Just Like Abraham Lincoln*
- *Miss Nelson Is Missing*
- *Sister Anne's Hands*
- *Thank You Mr. Falker*
- *Lily's Purple Plastic Purse*

Required Materials

- *Student Journal*, pages 15-1, 15-2, and 15-3
- Enough materials for each student to make the same product they practiced making in Lesson 14. Depending on what product the children are making you may use:
  - ➢ Rulers
  - ➢ Scissors
  - ➢ Crayons or colored markers
  - ➢ For Option C, hexaflexagon patterns and glue or stapler
- Homegram 15

Economics Background for Teachers

While there is no new economics material in this lesson, it expands the explanation of teachers as examples of human capital.

Vocabulary

- **Lesson Plan:** A plan that is developed ahead of time that provides the steps to teach something.

Preparation

Since *Treemonisha* is a long book, the teacher will have to begin many days in advance. The book is longer than the others in *Choices and Changes,* but it is rich in ideas related to many different areas of the curriculum. A possible service-learning activity would be for the students to perform the play for a younger class or a group of older citizens.

This day's activity is designed to give students experience in teaching another person. The Teaching Procedures suggest having students teach younger students how to make a paper puzzle, treasure box, or hexaflexagon. To prepare for this activity, it will be necessary to contact the teacher of a younger class and arrange a time when your students can teach the younger students. At least 30 minutes should be allowed for the teaching experience.

If it is not possible to arrange for your students to teach younger students, you may wish to follow the alternative teaching suggestion at the end of the Teaching Procedures in the lesson. The alternative suggests that the class be divided in half and that you teach the halves to make different origami (paperfolding) products. When the students have mastered the two products, they can teach each other how to make them.

Getting Started

1. Read *Treemonisha* and ask the following questions:

- When she was very young, what could Treemonisha do that no other black person for miles around could do? *(Read, write, and do her numbers.)*
- How did Treemonisha hope she could repay the community for their support of her education? *(She would teach their children.)*
- Why was Zodzetrick able to fool the people of Liberty? *(Because they were uneducated, they didn't have the human capital to see through his tricks. Zodzetrick used the power of other people's ignorance, while Treemonisha used the power of knowledge. Ignorance leads to misery and poverty; knowledge leads to power and many different types of wealth.)*
- Why did the people of Liberty think that Treemonisha would be a good leader? *(She was educated.)*

2. Read one of the other books listed above.

- Ask the students to describe the teacher in each book. *(If you read Just Like Abraham Lincoln, explain that many people are teachers outside a classroom.)*
- Ask the students to identify some people in their lives who have taught them things even though these people are not classroom teachers. *(Examples might include relatives, neighbors, or friends.)*
- What things did these people teach them? *(Examples might include riding a bike, tying their shoes.)*
- Ask students to identify some of the characteristics that made the teacher(s) in the story good teachers. *(Patience, kindness, perserverance, interest in the children, plenty of human capital, including knowledge of the material and the skill of teaching. Also, creativity and imagination.)*
- Tell the students that tomorrow they will take over your job; they are going to be teachers. Ask if they have ever thought of themselves as teachers. Explain that anyone who has a skill another person does not have can become a teacher to the unskilled person—if that person is willing to become the student. Ask the students if they have ever been a teacher to someone else. For example, have they ever taught a younger sister or brother to catch a ball, pour milk from the carton, or sing a song? Encourage volunteers to describe these experiences.

- Suggest that members of this class have a special skill they can teach a younger child: how to make the product they practiced making previously. Tell the students you have arranged for them to teach the students in another class. Before they meet their students, however, they must make a plan for teaching the skill.

Teaching Procedures

1. Distribute the *Student Journals* and have the students turn to page 15-1. On this page they will write down their plan for teaching their students. When they finish their teaching experience, they will describe on page 15-3 what they learned about teaching.

2. Help the students complete the first statement on page 15-1, which asks what they will teach. *(How to make the product.)*

3. Have them recall the skills and knowledge needed. List the responses on the chalkboard as they are given, and have the students copy them in their journals. *(Responses might include measuring, cutting, tracing, folding, gluing, and coloring.)*

4. Explain that younger students may not have all the knowledge and skills—the human capital—they have. Therefore, they may have to help the younger children learn to do some of the steps. Discuss the steps where help may be needed (perhaps measuring, tracing, or folding), and those that the younger students will probably be able to do on their own (cutting, gluing, coloring).

5. Tell the students it is important to develop a step-by-step lesson plan. Write the term "Lesson Plan" on the board. Review the word "plan," and explain that a lesson plan is a special type of plan that helps teachers in their work. It is a plan that is developed ahead of time, and it identifies the steps that will be used to teach something.

6. Help the students decide on the first step. Write the steps on the chalkboard as they are mentioned. Ordering steps sequentially is sometimes difficult for students at this age, so allow them to consider different possibilities and revise their first responses. Ultimately you may wish to reduce their responses to the six steps that appear in the following lists. You might want to write the directions on poster board if your students will visit younger children in another classroom.

7. You may use the directions from the book you have chosen or any of the three below:

- *Option A: Paper Puzzle*
  - ➢ Step 1. Cut out a square.
  - ➢ Step 2. Fold square in half both ways.
  - ➢ Step 3. Fold four corners to middle.
  - ➢ Step 4. Flip folded square and fold corners to middle.
  - ➢ Step 5. Place fingers in pockets and squeeze.
  - ➢ Step 6. Write numbers inside triangles.
- *Option B: Treasure Box*
  - ➢ Step 1. Cut out a square.
  - ➢ Step 2. Fold square in half both ways.
  - ➢ Step 3. Fold four corners to middle.
  - ➢ Step 4. Flip folded square and fold corners to middle.
  - ➢ Step 5. Fold out point of each triangle.
  - ➢ Step 6. Flip and fold out point of each square.
- *Option C: Hexaflexagon*
  - ➢ Step 1. Cut out a paper strip.
  - ➢ Step 2. Using the triangle pattern, trace 10 triangles on the strip.
  - ➢ Step 3. Score and crease the lines.
  - ➢ Step 4. Fold into a shape with six sides.
  - ➢ Step 5. Glue.
  - ➢ Step 6. Color.

8. Help the students decide which steps they will do for the younger students and which they will teach the students to do. Suggest they should bring along samples of the better products they made to show their students.

9. Have the students write the steps of their teaching plan on page 15-1 of their journals.

10. Before your students meet the younger students, remind them to follow some rules of good teaching:

- Tell the students your name.
- Learn the students' names and use them in calling on students.
- Be patient.
- Encourage the students by complimenting them.

11. Provide each of your students with the materials needed and take the class members to meet their "students." Remain available for questions, but allow your students to carry out their own teaching experience. (Allow at least 30 minutes for the teaching.) Instruct the "teachers" to let their students keep the finished products.

12. Upon returning to your classroom, encourage class members to share their teaching experiences. What steps were easy for their students? What steps were difficult? Did their students enjoy learning a new skill?

13. Turn your students' attention to their teaching. What was the easiest step to teach? What step was most difficult? What would they do differently if they were to teach someone else how to make the product?

14. Ask the students if they think their teaching experience improved their own human capital. If so, how? For example, did it make them think more about the easiest way to give clear directions?

15. Challenge the students to name other ways to improve their human capital. (Answers might include reading, listening to other people, and looking at pictures or diagrams.)

16. (**Optional**) Students might enjoy writing friendly letters to the children they taught, thanking them for their cooperation and encouraging them to continue to develop their skills and knowledge.

Assessment

1. Direct the students to complete page 15-3 in their journals. Have them describe what their students learned and did not learn; also have them describe what they learned about being a teacher. (*Answers might be that teaching is easy, difficult, fun, or frustrating.*) Tell the class that because one of a teacher's jobs is to give grades, they should give "grades" to their students and to themselves as teachers!

2. Show the students some help-wanted ads. Have them write a help-wanted ad for a teacher. Their ads should list the human capital that the teacher they would want to hire must possess.

Homegram

Distribute *Homegram 15*. Tell the students their teaching experience has prepared them to share their skills and knowledge with other people. Explain that the Homegram directs them to teach someone at home or in their neighborhood to make the product. Their "student" might be someone older or someone younger. To help your students remember the steps, they should copy them from page 15-1 of their journals onto the lower part of the Homegram page.

STUDENT JOURNAL Page 15-1
Teaching Others Builds Human Capital

I will be teaching my student how to make a _____ .

Some of the skills and knowledge I will have to teach my student are ____

_____

_____

This is my plan for teaching my student:

- Step 1 _____

- Step 2 _____

- Step 3 _____

- Step 4 _____

- Step 5 _____

- Step 6 _____

- Step 7 _____

- Step 8 _____

- Step 9 _____

- Step 10 _____

STUDENT JOURNAL Page 15-2
Teaching Others Builds Human Capital

Remember these guidelines for teaching:

- Tell the students your name.

- Learn the students' names and use their names in calling on them.

- Be patient.

- Encourage the students by complimenting them.

STUDENT JOURNAL Page 15-3
My Teaching Experience

My student's name was _____ .

My student improved his or her human capital by learning these skills and this knowledge: _____

_____

_____

_____

_____

I learned that being a teacher is _____

because _____

_____

_____

_____

_____

If I teach another student, I will improve my human capital by _____

_____

_____

_____

_____

The grade I would give my student is _____ .

The grade I would give myself as a teacher is _____ .

HOMEGRAM 15

Dear Homework Helper,

In the past few days, our class has learned how to make a product by using resources and a plan to produce an output. _____ is prepared to teach this skill to another person. Please follow the directions he or she gives to make the product.

Thank you for your help.

_____

_____

DIRECTIONS

Step 1 _____

Step 2 _____

Step 3 _____

Step 4 _____

Step 5 _____

Step 6 _____

Step 7 _____

Step 8 _____

Step 9 _____

Step 10 _____

UNIT FOUR
AN ECONOMY

UNIT FOUR
Overview: An Economy

The focus of Unit 4 is on the interdependence of buyers and sellers in the economy. Students learn about entrepreneurs and markets and then apply the principles of markets to labor markets. They learn that they will sell their human capital in labor markets.

Lesson 16. Entrepreneurs and the Interdependence of Buyers and Sellers

Students read *Mr. Blue Jeans*, the story of Levi Strauss, to learn the characteristics of an entrepreneur. They read *Pizza for Breakfast* to learn about the interdependence of buyers and sellers. They plan and conduct an interview of a businessperson from the community.

Lesson 17. Markets and Exchange

Students read *Amazon Boy* or *Market* to learn that a market is an interaction of buyers and sellers. They identify markets in which they and family members have participated. They learn that voluntary exchange benefits the traders and engage in an exchange activity in the classroom.

Lesson 18. The Labor Market: My Human Capital Pays Off

This is the final lesson of *Choices and Changes*. Students read *Oh, the Places You'll Go!* and select from a list of books to begin to envision their future role as workers/managers/ entrepreneurs in the economy. They review their skills inventory and compare it to skill requirements of jobs they might want. The class makes a wall size mural of each student as a future worker.

Lesson 16
Entrepreneurs and the Interdependence of Buyers and Sellers

What in the world is an entrepreneur?

Cognitive Objectives:

Students will

- Define *entrepreneur* as someone who takes risks and combines resources in new ways to produce goods and services.
- Define *consumption* as the act of using goods and services.
- Recognize the interdependence of consumers and producers.
- Identify specific questions to ask of specific business owners.
- Interview a business owner or business manager.

Affective Objectives:

Students will

- See entrepreneurs as people like themselves who have used their human capital to begin businesses.
- Recognize the importance of human capital in becoming an entrepreneur.

People often think of themselves as consumers, but not as producers. In this lesson, students will meet business owners, managers, and entrepreneurs so that they can identify with them and perhaps aspire to start their own businesses someday. Students should recognize that business owners depend on consumers to help them earn a living. Students should come away from this lesson realizing that "We are all in this together."

Required Books

* *Mr. Blue Jeans*
* *Mel's Diner*
* *Pizza for Breakfast*

Optional Books

* *Snowflake Bentley*
* *Once Upon a Company*
* *Arthur's Pet Business*
* *Arthur's Honey Bear*
* *Jalapeno Bagels*
* *A Busy Day at Mr. Kang's Groceries*
* *Mr. Santizo's Tasty Treats*

Required Materials

* A camera/film
* A tape recorder for each pair of students, if possible
* Activity 16-1
* *Student Journal*, pages 16-1, 16-2, 16-3
* One extra copy of page 16-2 in the *Student Journal*

Economics Background for Teachers

In this lesson, students learn about entrepreneurs and their businesses. They learn that people who own businesses take a risk and depend upon consumers to buy their products. In addition, entrepreneurs find new ways to combine resources to produce a product. Students also learn that consumers depend on businesses to supply the products they desire. This mutual dependence is both the strength and weakness of an economy where people specialize in the production of certain types of products and buy most of their products from others. This lesson will take two days, with the actual interviews on the second day.

Vocabulary

* **Alternative:** A possible choice; one of two or more possible actions or choices; opportunities from which people choose.
* **Choice:** A selection from two or more alternatives.
* **Consequence:** Something that happens as a result of an action or event.

- **Consumer:** A person whose wants are satisfied by using a good or service; a person who buys and uses goods and services.
- **Entrepreneur**: A person who organizes other productive resources, takes risks, and finds new ways of combining resources to produce a product.
- **Human capital:** The quality of labor resources which can be improved through investments in education, training, and health; skills and knowledge; also referred to as labor resources.
- **Innovation:** The introduction of an invention into a use that has economic value.
- **Interdependence:** Two or more persons or groups depending on each other.
- **Invention:** A new product.
- **Interview:** A meeting in which one person asks specific questions of another person to gather specific information.
- **Opportunity cost:** The value of the best alternative given up when a choice is made.
- **Physical capital:** Goods produced and used to produce other goods and services (capital resources.)
- **Production:** Using resources to produce a good or service.
- **Work:** Human physical or mental effort used in production of goods or services.

Teaching Procedures

DAY 1

Do this lesson; then give the students a week to think about their questions and to give the people who are going to be interviewed time to think about and prepare their answers. Also provide time for the students to practice with the tape recorders so that they know how to record.

1. Write the words "entrepreneur" and "innovation" on the board. Explain that "entrepreneur" is a long word, but it is one that you know they can learn. Ask the students to repeat the word. Explain that an entrepreneur is someone who takes risks and combines resources with a new and different plan. An entrepreneur introduces innovations. Ask the students to repeat "innovations." Explain that an innovation is a new way of producing a good or service.

2. Read *Mr. Blue Jeans*. (This is not a picture book, and it is longer than most of the books that have been used in *Choices and Changes*. It is the story of Levi Strauss and his entrepreneurship in creating, marketing, and selling Levis.) Give copies of Activity 16-1 to the students. Have them write their answers to the questions as you or they read the book.

- What service did Levi Strauss provide when he arrived in New York? *(He was a peddler, selling goods to people in New York. Later, he went out into the country.)*
- Where did Levi go after New York? *(Kentucky.)*
- Where did he go next? *(San Francisco.)*
- What did he do there? *(He worked with his brother-in-law in the dry goods business.)*
- What was Levi's first innovation? *(Canvas pants.)*
- What was his second innovation? *(The rivets.)*
- Describe some of the characteristics that made Levi Strauss a successful entrepreneur. *(He was creative, innovative, persevering, hard working, brave.)*
- Can you think of any other famous entrepreneurs? *(Possibilities include Famous Amos, Mrs. Fields, Bill Gates, Thomas Edison.)*

3. **(Optional for advanced classes)** Read *Once Upon a Company*. This is also longer than most of the books previously recommended, and it is very advanced; but it provides the students with a true example of children who are entrepreneurs. If you use this book, break it up and read a chapter from time to time.

4. Write the words "Producer" and "Consumer" on the board with two arrows— one pointing from consumer to producer and one from producer to consumer.

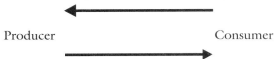

Producer   Consumer

Remind the students that they have been studying production, and they know that producers make goods and services. Explain that consumers use goods and services and pay producers for their products. Explain that these two groups are interdependent. Write the word "interdependent" on the board; explain that people or groups are interdependent when they depend upon one another other. For example, consumers depend on producers to provide the goods and services they want, and producers depend on consumers to buy the products they produce, thus providing them with income.

5. Read *Pizza for Breakfast*.

- Ask the students to identify the producers and the consumers in the story. *(Frank and Zelda and the waiters are producers. Frank and Zelda produce a good, the pizza, while the waiters produce a service, bringing the orders to Frank and Zelda and the pizzas to the consumers. The consumers include the factory workers, then "the man," then the basketball team, then many more people.)*
- Ask the students why Frank and Zelda were so unhappy when the factory closed. *(They had no customers for their pizza parlor.)*

- Ask the students how did Frank and Zelda depend on the factory workers. *(The factory workers bought the pizza and provided income for Frank and Zelda.)*
- Ask the students how did people depend on Frank and Zelda. *(They wanted the pizza that Frank and Zelda made.)*
- Point to the words "producer" and "consumer" on the board and explain that the arrows mean that producers depend on consumers and consumers depend on producers.

6. Read *Mel's Diner.*

- Ask the students how did Mabel's parents get Mel's Diner. *(They bought it from Mel.)*
- Ask the students to think of some of the advantages of owning their own business. *(You are your own boss; you can run a business that you like; you can have your children come to work with you.)*
- Ask the students to think of the disadvantages. *(The owners work very long hours; they can't spend much time with Mabel outside the diner.)*

7. Ask the students how Levi Strauss was different from Frank and Zelda or Mabel's parents? *(He found new ways to produce products.)* Explain that entrepreneurs do more than take risks in owning or managing businesses; they also find new ways of providing goods and services. (Similar questions can be asked for any of the other books listed above.)

8. **(Optional)** The Thank You Game

- One sign of the interdependence of producers and consumers is the fact that people often say "Thank you" after purchasing something, and salespeople often say "Thank you" after selling something.
- Have your students say "Thank you very much" when they are helped by salespeople. Have your students report to the class on instances when the salesperson did or did not say "Thank you" back. The mutual "Thank you" illustrates the interdependence of buyers and sellers.

9. This day's activity will provide preparation for the business interviews suggested for DAY 2 of this lesson. Because the purpose of the interviews is to give the students an opportunity to hear about actual experiences of adult business owners in their work and their personal lives, several interviewees should be available for the interviews. The interviewees should be business owners from the community. Preferably, the students will be able to suggest some business people to interview.

10. The students should conduct their interviews in pairs. The number of interviewees you contact should be at least a third the number of pairs in your

class. For example, if you have 30 students (15 pairs) in class, you may wish to arrange for five adults to be interviewed. Each interviewee can then be interviewed by three pairs of students.

11. When contacting potential interviewees, explain that the purpose of the interviews will be to personalize and make more real the concepts students have been studying in *Choices and Changes*. In particular, students will be interested in questions similar to those listed in Procedure 15 of this lesson. Give the interviewees a copy of the questions beforehand and make yourself available to answer any questions they may have.

12. Agree on the date and time for the interviewees to visit the classroom. If you plan to take photos of the interviews, remember to bring a camera and film.

13. Tell the students that they have been learning about production. In *Pizza for Breakfast* they learned about running a business and the fact that business managers have to have customers in order to keep the business running. To help them understand businesses better, you would like them to interview some business people from the community. Ask for suggestions about business people they might interview. To the extent that you can, use the students' suggestions and contact the people to ask them if they would be willing to be interviewed by the students.

14. Remind the students that when they studied human capital, they learned that one way to build skills and knowledge is to talk with other people. In DAY 2 of this lesson they will be talking to other people, but you would like their conversation to be more than just a friendly chat. Instead they are to conduct an interview. Ask the students if they know what an interview is. If they are unsure, remind them of interviews they may have seen on television news programs. Write the word "interview" on the board and explain that an interview involves asking another person specific questions in order to gather specific information. Tell the students that the main difference between a friendly conversation and an interview is that the person leading the interview has prepared questions ahead of time. The more specific the questions, the more information will be learned during the interview. Explain that the students' task today is to decide what questions to ask in their interviews.

15. Describe the people to be interviewed. Briefly describe their jobs and anything else about their lives that would be useful to the students in developing questions.

16. Through discussion, develop and list on the chalkboard a series of questions that should be asked in each interview. The list might include the following interview questions:

- What kind of business do you run?
- Do you produce a good or provide a service? Please describe the good or service.
- How long have you owned/managed the business?
- Why did you choose that business?
- Did you take a risk when you began your business? What type of risk?
- How does your good or service differ from similar goods or services provided by others?
- How do you get customers to buy your good or service?
- Do you know anyone whose business has not attracted customers? If so, what happened to them?
- What have you given up in order to run your business? What else could you be doing?
- How many workers work for you?
- What capital resources do you use in your business? Computers? Machines? Buildings?
- How do the resources help you do your work faster, better, or more easily?
- Describe your human capital. (What skills and knowledge do you have that help you in running your business?)
- How does your human capital improve as a result of your work in running your business?
- Do you use creativity in your business?
- What is one major choice that you made in your life?
- What changes in your life—good and bad—resulted from that major choice?
- When you made that choice, what was the opportunity cost? (What did you have to give up?)
- What is the best part of running your business?
- What is the hardest part?
- What advice would you give me for my life?

In addition to these general questions you may wish to help the students develop specific questions about the businesses, such as: What kind of school or training is required? What other kinds of businesses could you run with those skills? Type or write these questions.

17. Distribute the *Student Journals* and have the students turn to page 16-1. Tell them that everyone will take part in the interviews (they may work in pairs or groups, depending on what will work best in your situation; but make sure that all the students will be able to ask at least one or two questions). Assign the pairs or groups; then have the groups decide what questions they want to ask the person they interview. Students should write the questions they want to ask in their journals on page 16-2. During the interview each will be responsible for asking

these questions and for recording the answers given by the person interviewed. Draw attention to the **Things to Remember to Do in My Interview** list at the bottom of the page, and be sure students read the list.

18. Remind the students that one way to improve their human capital is to practice. To prepare for the interview, have one pair of students interview you, preparing the questions they wish to ask you on the extra copy of page 16-2 of the *Student Journal.* Make certain they remember to introduce themselves, learn your name, listen carefully, and thank you at the end of the interview. Have the students practice writing down your answers on a separate sheet of paper. Encourage them to take turns when asking questions so that one student can be writing the answer to the last question while another is asking the next question. If the students have difficulty writing neatly during the interview, suggest that they rewrite the answers when the interview is over. (Another way to do this is to have the students tape record the interview, if you have access to enough tape recorders.) Another practice option involves having pairs of students interview one another. In these practice interviews, allow the students to assume roles of any workers they wish. Tell them they need to be familiar with the job they choose so that they can answer questions about it. You may prefer to work with pictures to help them in the practice interviews.

19. Encourage the students to change or add to the questions they plan to ask in the actual interviews, based on their practice experience.

20. Explain that during the interviews the following day, they will have to take turns interviewing the visiting workers. While they are waiting, they can observe other students interviewing someone with whom they also will speak. This will allow them to learn from more than one adult worker. Caution them to listen quietly and not interrupt while they are observing.

DAY 2
Preparation

Before the arrival of the adults who will be interviewed, arrange the classroom into interview areas. Make certain there is enough space between interview areas to eliminate distractions for the interviewers and interviewees. Get your camera ready.

Getting Started

Before the interviewees arrive, distribute the *Student Journals* and have the students review the questions they prepared to ask (on page 16-2 of their journals). Remind them that they may find it easier to write answers on a separate sheet first and then rewrite them neatly later. Review interview guidelines. Recall the **Things to Remember to Do in My Interview** on page 16-1 of the *Student Journals*. If the students are working in groups, assign each group one of the adult workers to interview.

Teaching Procedure

1. Introduce the adult interviewees to the students, and have the students escort the guests to their assigned areas. Let the students take the lead in conducting the interviews. If the adults will be interviewed by more than one group of students, decide how much time to allot for each interview, and announce when it is time to change interviewers. (About 15 minutes per interview should be allowed. If you are taking photos of the interviews, try to get one photo of each group of students.)

2. When all the groups have finished, have the students thank the interviewees before they leave. Allow the students time to rewrite their answers to the questions on page 16-2 of their *Student Journals*.

3. Invite the students to tell about their interview experiences. If they do not mention some of the concepts covered in *Choices and Changes* (goods and services, physical and human capital, choices, production, alternatives, opportunity cost, consequences), help them relate some of the answers they received to these concepts. From the discussion, help the students draw some generalizations and write the generalizations on the chalkboard. They should include conclusions such as these:

- Education is important because it helps develop human capital needed for work and for life.
- Owning a business is hard work.
- Owning a business requires a great deal of human capital.
- Owning a business is risky.
- Businesses depend on customers.

Assessment

Distribute the *Student Journals* and have the students turn to page 16-3. Explain that this page allows them to sum up what they learned in the interviews. If you plan to provide photos, tell the students they can glue them in later. If the students are to draw a picture of the person they interviewed, allow them time to do so.

Have the students share their feelings about how the information from the interviews may relate to their own goals and plans for the future. For example, did they learn that running a business might require more training or education than they had considered? Did they learn that running a business is risky and a lot of work?

STUDENT JOURNAL Page 16-1
Some Questions I Can Ask

- What kind of business do you run?

- Do you produce a good or provide a service? Please describe the good or service.

- How does your good or service differ from similar goods or services provided by others?

- How long have you owned/managed the business?

- Why did you choose that business?

- Did you take a risk when you began your business? What type of risk?

- How do you get customers to buy your good or service?

- What would happen if customers stopped buying your product?

- Do you know anyone whose business has not attracted customers? If so, what happened to them?

- What have you given up in order to run your business? What else could you be doing?

- How many workers work for you?

- What capital resources do you use in your business? Computers? Machines? Buildings?

- How do these resources help you do your work faster, better, or more easily?

- Describe your human capital. (What skills and knowledge do you have that help you in running your business?)

- How does your human capital improve as a result of your work in running your business?

- What is one major choice that you made in your life?

- What changes in your life—good and bad—resulted from that choice?

- When you made that choice, what was the opportunity cost? (What did you have to give up?)

- What is the best part of running your business?
- What is the hardest part?
- What advice would you give me for my life?
- Other questions:

_____

_____

_____

Interviewing Entrepreneurs

Things to Remember to Do in My Interview:

❏ Introduce myself.

❏ Listen carefully.

❏ Write down the answers I hear.

❏ Thank the person I interview.

STUDENT JOURNAL Page 16-2
Planning and Conducting My Interview

Question _____

Answer _____

_____

_____

_____

Question _____

Answer _____

_____

_____

_____

Question _____

Answer _____

_____

_____

_____

Question _____

Answer _____

_____

_____

_____

Question _____

Answer _____

_____

_____

_____

STUDENT JOURNAL Page 16-3
Remembering My Interview

This is a picture of the person I interviewed.

The important lessons I learned from this interview are:

_____

_____

_____

_____

_____

_____

_____

_____

_____

_____

ACTIVITY 16-1
The Story of Levi Strauss

1. What service did Levi Strauss provide when he arrived in New York?

2. Where did Levi go after New York?

3. Where did he go next?

4. What did he do there?

5. What was Levi's first innovation?

6. What was his second innovation?

7. Describe some of the characteristics that made Levi Strauss a successful entrepreneur.

8. Can you think of any other famous entrepreneurs?

Lesson 17
Markets and Exchange
What is a market, and why do you care?

Cognitive Objectives:

Students will

- Define a *market* as an interaction of buyers and sellers.
- Recognize that both parties gain from voluntary exchange.
- Identify goods and services that they buy through markets.

Affective Objective:

Students will

- Feel empowered when they make voluntary exchanges.

Required Book

- *Amazon Boy* or *Market*

Optional Books

- *To Market, To Market*
- *Markets: From Barter to Bar Codes*
- *Beneath the Stone*
- *Don't Leave an Elephant to Go and Chase a Bird*

Required Materials

- *Student Journal*, page 17-1
- Exchange box
- Items for the exchange box
- Homegram 17

Economics Background for Teachers

People often confuse markets with places. While a market may be held in a place, it is essentially an interaction of buyers and sellers. Usually, in this interaction, buyers and sellers exchange goods and services for money, but they may trade goods and services for other goods and services (this is called bartering). These exchanges of goods, services, and money may occur in a place or through interaction by telephone, mail, or the Internet.

When people engage in a voluntary exchange, they do so because both parties expect to gain from the exchange. When people buy gasoline, regardless of the price, they must expect that their benefit from the gasoline they buy is greater than the cost of buying it—or else they would not have bought it. Often people will say that they *had to* purchase the gas because they had to get to work. The economist replies that they must have valued getting to work more than the cost of the gas. People may not like the price of a good or service when they purchase it, but their act of purchasing suggests that they value the good or service more highly than the price they pay.

Vocabulary

- **Market:** An interaction of buyers and sellers.

Preparation

At least one week before you begin this lesson, you will need to prepare an "Exchange Box." This "Exchange Box" can be a simple cardboard box without any decoration, or you can cover it with colored paper and decorate it. It must be large enough to hold the items that the students bring to class *(See Homegram 17)*. You will want to give the students ample time to bring these goods in. Have the Exchange Box ready for the students' goods by the time that you send out the Homegram.

Getting Started

Draw the following schematic on the board:

Money

Buyers   Market   Sellers

Goods and Services

Explain that a market is an interaction of buyers and sellers; it provides a way for buyers and sellers to exchange goods and services and money. While a market may be a place, often it is not. Explain that buyers and sellers often exchange goods and services and money over the telephone, by mail, on the Internet, or from a friend or acquaintance. Tell the students that a market exists, for example, when repair people sell their services in a home, repairing appliances. Explain that there are markets for all kinds of goods and services: as long as there is a buyer, a seller, and something to exchange, there is a market.

Teaching Procedures

1. Tell the students that you are going to read them a story about different markets. Ask them to name different products that they hear referred to in the story. Make a list of these products on the board. Read *Amazon Boy* or *Market*. (Both are likely to have vocabulary with which your students are unfamiliar. Prepare a list of vocabulary items as necessary and be ready to explain them to the students as you read the story.)

2. Explain that there are two types of people who participate in markets–buyers and sellers. Buyers come because they hope to find things they want to buy; sellers come to sell the goods that they produce or buy from others. Often people come to markets to buy and to sell.

3. Ask the students to help you make a list of goods and services they have purchased or seen purchased lately. Their list will undoubtedly include food items, but encourage them to think of other goods and services. Write their suggestions on the board.

- Ask them to tell you whether the goods and services they identify were purchased at a store, by telephone, by mail, over the Internet, or from a friend or acquaintance. Write an "S," "T," "M," "I," or "F" for the categories above. (If the students don't know, put a question mark next to the good or service.)
- Ask where all of these goods and services come from. Some students will know about some particular items, but the general answer is that people come from all over to supply goods and services to the market. They are the suppliers. Some of them produce the goods; others buy them from someone else. Markets provide a way for buyers and sellers to get together to exchange goods and services.
- Today students will learn about exchange and markets, and the reasons people have for participating in markets.

4. Distribute the *Student Journals*. Ask the students to turn to page 17-1. There they should copy (from the chalkboard summary) the list of goods and services

they have seen exchanged and how the good was purchased (S, T, M, I, or F.) Ask the students why they think people brought these goods to the market. Help them to see that the people want to sell them so that they can earn money to buy things they want. The people who bring these goods to market are much like the entrepreneurs that the students interviewed earlier. They produce goods in the hope that others will buy them. The market allows them to find buyers for their products so that they can buy other products.

5. Ask the students to bring a good from home to class. This should be a small item, under $5 in value; it should be something that belongs to the student and something he or she no longer wants. Be sure to explain that each student's Homework Helper must sign the Homegram stating what the item is and that the student has permission to bring it to school.

6. Read *Don't Leave an Elephant to Go and Chase a Bird.*

- Have the students list all the exchanges that Anancy Spiderman made. Ask them why he continued to exchange things. *(He always traded for something that he valued more highly.)*
- Except for the elephants, why did the others with whom he traded exchange? *(They valued what they were getting more highly than what they were giving up.)*

7. Ask the students to place their items in the Exchange Box that you have placed in the front of the room. Explain that you will not be able to play the Exchange Game until everyone has brought an item. Have some small items available, such as candy or inexpensive toys, for those who can't bring in an item. Let the students know that these are available, but that they must speak with you if they are unable to bring an item.

8. Once every student has an item in the box, you are ready to play the game. Distribute the items from the Exchange Box randomly to the class. Tell the students that they are going to choose from two alternatives. They may keep the item that they have or they may trade with someone. Ask each student to explain what he or she has to the class. Each student should take no more than about 30 seconds to do this.

9. Open up the classroom to exchange. Students who wish to do so may exchange their good with another student. Emphasize the fact that they are not required to exchange. They will have five minutes to trade, and may make as many exchanges as they wish.

10. Once five minutes have elapsed, have the students take their seats. Ask them to raise their hands if they exchanged more than once. Ask those who did so to

explain what they exchanged and with whom. Then call on some "exchange partners" to explain why they traded. Help them to see that they both were better off after the exchange because they gained a good that they valued more than the good they gave up.

11. Ask people who did not exchange to raise their hands. Ask them why they did not trade. Most will say that there was nothing worth trading for. Explain that exchange only works if two people expect to gain from it.

12. Thank the students and tell them that they may keep the items they have.

13. Explain that the exchanges that take place in markets are similar to those they have just completed in class. The difference is that in most markets buyers and sellers use money. But buyers and sellers make exchanges in markets because they expect to gain from their trades. A "ripoff" can't occur if both traders go into the exchange with good information.

Assessment

Ask the students to look at the list of goods and services that they listed on page 17-1 in their student journals. What do the buyers have to give up to buy the goods or services? Remind them of the concept of opportunity cost. *(Buyers give up money that they could have used to buy something else.)* Ask them why they or their friends or parents buy things. *(Because they value what they buy more than they value the opportunity cost—just as the students valued what they gained in the exchange activity more than they valued what they gave up.)*

STUDENT JOURNAL Page 17-1

Goods and Services That I Have Seen Exchanged

Items	Method of Exchange

HOMEGRAM 17

Dear Homework Helper,

In class this week we are learning about markets and exchange. I have asked your student to bring an item to class that he or she is willing to exchange. This should be something that is no longer wanted by you or the student. It should be worth no more than $5 but may be worth less. Students will bring these items into class and put them in our Exchange Box. On the day of the Exchange Game, I will distribute these items randomly to the students. They will then have an opportunity to trade their item for any other item from the Exchange Box. The purpose of this game is to help students understand that both participants in an exchange gain when people trade with full information.

Please help your student decide what to bring to class and complete the form below.

Thank you.

_____

_____

With my permission, _____
                          Student's Name

has decided to bring a(n) _____
to class for the Exchange Game.

Signed _____

Lesson 18

The Labor Market:
My Human Capital Pays Off

What will I be when I grow up?

Cognitive Objectives:

Students will

- Identify buyers and sellers in labor markets.
- List reasons why employers hire workers.
- List reasons why workers supply labor.
- Identify roles that they may play in labor markets in the future.
- Identify one action step necessary to prepare for their roles in the labor market.
- Participate with other students in envisioning future success for all class members.
- List human capital required to succeed in a future job of their own.

Affective Objective:

Students will

- Envision themselves as future workers, business owners or managers, professionals, or entrepreneurs.

Required Book

- *Oh, the Places You'll Go*

Optional Books

- *Amazing Grace*
- *Jeremy's Choice*
- *Robert the Rose Horse*
- *Story Painter: The Life of Jacob Lawrence*
- *Strega Nona*
- *The Art Lesson*
- *Oliver Button Is a Sissy*
- *At the Crossroads*
- *Calling the Doves*
- *Fly Away Home*
- *My Old Man*
- *The Wagon*
- *Voices from the Fields*
- *Working Cotton*
- *Plays of People at Work*

Required Materials

- Student Journal, pages 18-1, 18-2, 18-3, 18-4, 9-1

- Wall-size mural paper
- Colored marking pens or watercolor paints

Economics Background for Teachers

A labor market is similar to a product market in that each involves buyers and sellers. The buyers in a labor market are employers, and the sellers are employees. One of the most important lessons that students should learn early in life is that employers hire workers only if they expect those workers to add to their profits. In order to add to an employer's profits (and to make themselves valuable in the labor market), workers must have human capital. As emphasized throughout *Choices and Changes,* one of the ways to improve human capital is to gain knowledge and skills in school.

Vocabulary

- **Labor market**: An interaction of people who want to work and people who want to hire workers.

Review as necessary: Alternatives, Choices, Human Capital, Knowledge, Markets, Work

---

Getting Started

Tell the students that today they will start the last lesson of *Choices and Changes*. In this lesson they will discuss how they will "get on their way," and where they think they want to go as workers.

Read one or more of the optional books listed above. Ask the children to list some of the careers the characters chose or careers listed in the books. List these careers on the board. How did the characters work to achieve their career goals? *(They learned and practiced.)* If your students wanted to work in these careers, what human capital would help them achieve their goal?

Remind the students of their interviews with business owners and managers. Discuss the alternatives those adults had in choosing their business. Also remind the students of their discussion in Lesson 7 about the work people do. Emphasize that most people make choices about the work they do, but their alternatives are determined, to a large extent, by the human capital that they have developed. To have the widest possible range of alternatives, they must develop skills and knowledge that will allow them to do many different jobs.

Review the concepts of buyers, sellers, and markets. Explain to the children that they will one day participate in a labor market. Write the words "labor market" on the board. Explain that a labor market is like other markets except that in a labor market people are buying and selling workers' services. A labor market is an interaction of people who want to work and people who want to hire workers.

Teaching Procedures

1. Ask the students why employers hire workers. Using any of the optional books in this lesson that apply, or any in the previous lessons, ask the children to identify employers and ask why the employers hire the workers. Why do the business owners and managers that they interviewed hire workers? *(Because workers help employers produce their good or service and thus provide them income.)* What does that say about the workers who get hired? *(They must work hard to help the business run well.)*

2. Distribute the *Student Journals* and ask the students to turn to page 18-1. Have them use the books listed above to make a list of six jobs they think they would like to have in the future. Explain that these are alternatives from which they may choose. Now ask them to list the skills and knowledge they think they will need to succeed in these careers. (Optional: If they are not sure what the job requirements are, encourage them to find out by going to the library and having the librarian

help them look up the job in a book from the career shelf or by talking with someone who does the job.)

3. Return to Lesson 6 and review the decision-making process with the children.

4. **(Optional)** Use *Plays of People at Work* to prepare four skits. Have the students present the plays at a parent night. You might want to hold the parent night after the students have made the mural, but begin getting ready now. Allow the students to consider the different plays and use the decision-making apron to choose the four you will present.

5. Have the students narrow their career alternatives down to two; then they should use the decision-making apron shown on page 18-2 of their journals to decide which career they would choose. Explain that this choice doesn't limit them; they are likely to have many different careers and jobs in their lives. What steps will they take in school and out of school to acquire these skills?

6. Tell the students to turn to page 18-3 in their journals. This is their dream page. On it they are to draw portraits of themselves as future workers based on Step 5 above. Point out that most people have more than one job in a lifetime, so this might not be their only one. In their drawing they should show themselves doing something in that job. For example, they might be fighting a fire with a hose, icing a cake in a bakery, taking a patient's temperature, operating a computer, flying an airplane, arguing a case in court, operating on a patient, teaching a class of students. Beneath their portraits students should write their own name and the name of the job they have drawn.

7. Tell the students that they are going to create a wall mural of themselves (the whole class) as future workers. Tell them to mark off the paper into sections and assign a section to each student. (If you don't have room for one whole mural, you can cut the paper for each student ahead of time.) On the mural paper, each student should draw her/himself as a future worker, and then color her/his own portrait. Then have the group work together to color or paint the areas between the portraits so the mural looks like one large picture.

8. When the mural is finished, compliment the students on their work and have them tell what they see in the picture. Help them realize that each of them has choices in life and that they can increase the quantity and quality of the alternatives available to them as workers if they continue to increase their human capital.

9.Tell them that you are going to read a very special book. Ask them to think about their lives in the future as you read the book. Read *Oh, the Places You'll Go*.

- The book mentions "not-so-good streets." Ask the students what "not-so-good" streets they are too smart to go down.
- The book says "You'll start happening too." Ask them what they think "You'll start happening too" means. *(There are plenty of interpretations, but it probably means that they will start taking more control of their lives.)*
- The book mentions "soaring to new heights." Ask the students to describe what it feels like to be "soaring to high heights." Ask them if they have ever "been in a slump" and what that feels like.
- Ask the students how the lessons they've learned in *Choices and Changes* help when, "Simple it's not, I'm afraid you will find, for a mind-maker-upper to make up his mind," or when they're in the "waiting place"?
- When you read the last page in the book, ask the students how *Choices and Changes* can help them "get on their way."

Assessment

1. Have the students complete page 18-4 in their journals, listing the human resources required in the jobs of their choice. Have them compare that list of skills to the skills and knowledge they listed previously on page 9-1 of their journals. Can they add to the list on page 9-1? If so, the added items indicate what they have learned since they begin to keep track of their human capital.

2. Have the students describe a step they must take to reach their long-term job goal. The step might require long-term effort—in order to finish high school, for example. Or the step might be a shorter one, such as to learning how to count change or to add and subtract without using a pencil. If the students are willing, encourage them to share their future-worker goals with the class. Help them think about obstacles that exist and how the obstacles might be overcome.

3. Have the students write a letter of recommendation for any of the characters in any of the books you and the children have read. Explain that they can use the Human Capital Checklist (Activity 10-1) to explain to the future employer why he or she should want to hire the character. Help them understand that the skills and knowledge in question are the things people will list when writing letters of recommendation for them.

STUDENT JOURNAL Page 18-1

Careers and Skills

Careers I Might Like	Necessary Skills and Knowledge

STUDENT JOURNAL Page 18-2
The Decision-Making Apron

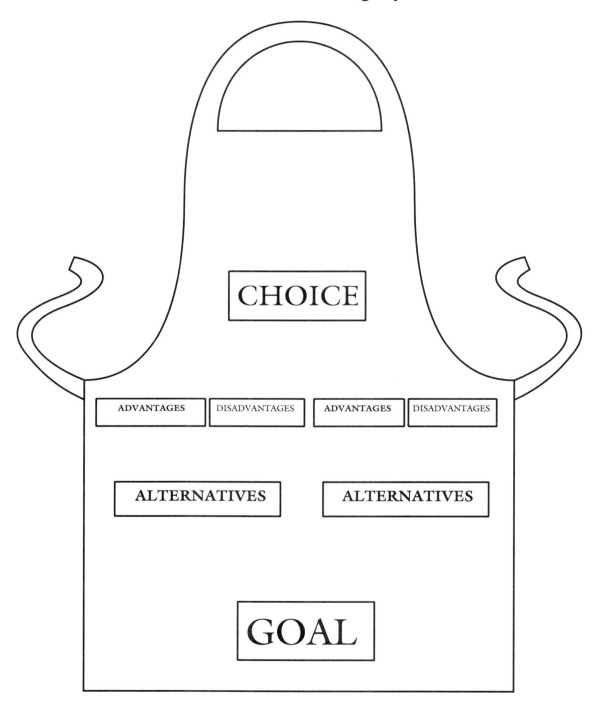

STUDENT JOURNAL Page 18-3

Me As a Worker/Entrepreneur

STUDENT JOURNAL PAGE 18-4
Skills and Knowledge I Will Use in My Career

My plan to acquire those skills and this knowledge.

The Service-Learning Project

A service-learning project is an integral part of *Choices and Changes*. As students learn about making decisions, they learn that economic decisions can be used to help others, not merely to improve their own situation. Toward this end, some *Choices and Changes* lessons have specific service-learning objectives.

Students should understand that service learning is not simply doing something for others. In a successful service-learning project, students ***learn*** by doing a ***service*** for someone else. Both the service for others and the new learning are essential for a successful project.

Steps to Accomplish the Project

1. Use the five-step decision-making process to choose a project.
2. Identify the human capital and other resources that will be used in the project.
3. Develop a plan for the project:
   a. Identify the tasks (work) to be done.
   b. Identify the people who will do each task.
   c. Check with the people for whom the work will be done.
   d. Establish deadlines for each task.
4. Carry out the project.
5. Assess the effectiveness of the project (reflection):
   a. Did the work get done?
   b. Did the work get done on time?
   c. Did the people for whom it was done seem to enjoy it? How did the service benefit those for whom or with whom it was done?
   d. What did the students learn from doing the project? What economics did they learn? What did they learn about themselves? What did they learn about their classmates? What did they learn about (or from) those for (or with) whom they did the project?
   e. What would the class do differently to improve the project?

The Process within *Choices and Changes*

You may begin the project after Unit One, or you may choose to wait until Unit Four; by that time students will have seen many more alternatives and will understand more about production. Waiting will also give the students an opportunity to use step 5 of the decision-making process, "Re-evaluate your choice." There is a trade-off between beginning the project early, when the students may lack sufficient knowledge of production, and beginning it later, when they will benefit from prior work with *Choices and Changes* but may also be constrained by a shortage of time remaining in the year. Another way to use the service-learning project is to begin early and then draw upon the students' experience with it to reinforce subsequent *Choices and Changes* lessons.

Lesson 1

Students begin thinking of service-learning projects they might do. Tell the students that scarcity affects everyone. Tell them that their class will identify a project to benefit the school or community, through minimizing the problem of scarcity in a particular case. They should begin thinking of appropriate possibilities for this project. Do an informal assessment of the wants of the community (including the school). Brainstorm things that would improve the school that are not provided by the administration. Or you might do a more formal assessment that could include a survey or interviews.

Lesson 2

Students consider alternatives for their project. You may want to wait until Unit 4 to actually decide on the service-learning project. Do, however, have the students begin to look at some possible projects so that they can be thinking about it as they progress through *Choices and Changes*. Explain to the students that they will identify some alternatives for their service-learning project. Present the list of alternatives and tell them that they are welcome to add to the list at any time. They should talk this over with adults at home and elsewhere to see what alternatives they can identify.

When you begin to choose a project, have the students look at the list of alternatives and identify groups or individuals for whom they could provide a service. Some possibilities include the students' friends or relatives, the school, the community, the aged, or the homeless. Narrow those alternatives down to three or four. Then have the class identify things that they could do for the individuals or groups. There are really two questions: for whom do you want to provide a good or service and what do you want to do for them? You can begin with either. For example, the class might decide that they want to do something for the homeless; then they could decide what to do. Or, they might decide that they want to make a quilt and then decide what type of quilt and for whom.

Have the students turn to page 2-3 in their *Student Journals* and complete an alternative tree for their service-learning project.

Lesson 3

Students narrow their alternatives down to two. To help the students narrow the list, map out a list of advantages and disadvantages of each alternative.

Lesson 5

Students identify the opportunity cost of choosing either of the two alternatives.

Lesson 6

Students use the five-step decision-making process to choose a service-learning project. (They may re-evaluate their decision after completing later lessons.) Put on the decision-making apron or go to the poster on the bulletin board or use the decision-making transparency. Tell the students that they are going to use the five steps to decide on their service-learning project. The alternatives are those that have been discussed. Have them list the two alternatives they have proposed and review the advantages and disadvantages of each. Have them vote on the projects. Once the choice has been identified, tell the students that they will have an opportunity to rethink their decision to see if they still think it is a good one. Explain that the benefit of their choice is the value of all the advantages they have listed. The cost of their choice is what they gave up—the alternative not chosen.

Have the students turn to page 6-2 in their *Student Journals*. Ask them to answer the questions on the page, describing how they identified their choice concerning the service-learning project.

Lessons 7 and 8

Students identify the tasks for the project. They begin making a plan for doing the work, listing the steps that will be taken.

Lesson 9

Students add to the plan by identifying the human capital that will be used in the project. They start to identify other people (other teachers, parents or other adults at home: people they know with special types of human capital which would be useful in the project) who may be asked to help with the project.

Lesson 10

Students identify ways in which their service-learning project amounts to an investment in their human capital.

Lesson 11

Students continue to develop their plan by identifying other resources that will be required for the project. They also identify sources for acquiring those other resources.

Lesson 12

Students use the decision-making apron and decide if they want to stay with the project they have chosen or select a different one. Once they make a final choice, they continue to plan, producing a written statement of the expected output and the inputs needed.

Students now know enough about resources and production to begin production of their service-learning project, whether it involves a good or a service. Once they decide what the output will be, help them identify the resources that will be used and the production plan. What activities will be done, who will be contacted, who will gather the resources, who will do the producing? Will the class want to ask some adults to lend their human capital to the process?

Once the production plan is developed, help the students to assign tasks to individuals and set deadlines for each stage of the project. *Chato's Kitchen* can be used to help the students see what is involved in planning a party. Whether their primary project involves a party or not, have them bring in their cooked products for a party for different grades, or for a visit to a homeless shelter or some other group.

Lesson 14

Students consider whether they want to make a class quilt. Review the information about quilting in Lesson 6. Read *Eight Hands Round, The Keeping Quilt*, and *The Patchwork Quilt*. Ask the students if they would like to make a quilt based on *Eight Hands Round*. Suggest that if they made the quilt they could give it to students in a lower grade who could use it to help them learn their alphabet letters. Suggest that they might want to use the patterns in *Eight Hands Round* with the patterns and letters for each pattern on the patches. This is one alternative for their service-learning project. Once the quilt is complete, each student in the class could teach one letter and explain the pattern to students in the lower grade. (Most communities have a quilting society. Check with the city library or look for the American Quilter's Society (AQS) on the web (http://www.aqsquilt.com/) or call (270-898-7903) to identify a guild near you.)

Lesson 15

A possible service-learning activity would be for the students to perform the play *Treemonisha* for a younger class or a group of older citizens.

Lesson 17

Students identify ways in which their service-learning project improved their human capital and improved the condition of the larger community (mutual benefit).

Some Tips for Providing Services

- Treat those you are "helping" with respect. Be considerate of their pride.
- Many of these projects can be done **with** people instead of **for** them.
- If you are dealing with senior citizens, be very careful not to treat them as children.
- Consult with the people you are going to help before beginning the project and after the project is completed.

Groups for Whom You Might Do a Service-Learning Project

- Younger children
- Children or adults in the hospital
- Families in homeless shelters
- Senior citizens
- People living in poverty
- Any of the above who are friends or relatives of students in the class

Suggested Projects and the Lessons to Which They Apply

- Plant a school garden. (Lesson 3)
- Develop respect for others by creating a cultural awareness program through reading, food, art, and clothing. Make one day each month a cultural awareness day. (Lesson 5)
- Bake some goods at home and bring them to a homeless shelter, a food kitchen, or some other group, or use them for a staff appreciation day. (Lesson 12)
- Invite older relatives and other senior citizens to the classroom. Have them share with students the story of their cultural heritage, upbringing, and interaction with other Americans. Give the guests simple gifts the students have made ahead of time. Make a book or a quilt of the stories and experiences. Invite the guests back for a "sharing" evening and prepare baked goods to entertain your guests. (Lesson 5, 10, 12, 14)
- Have a bake sale and use the money you earn to buy and deliver a holiday meal basket containing ham, turkey, roast beef, or other main course, canned vegetables, or food appropriate for particular cultures and their holidays. (Lesson 5, 12, 16, 17)
- Compile a cookbook composed of kid-friendly or multicultural recipes from parents and other adults. Reproduce and distribute the cookbooks to other classes. (Lesson 5, 12)
- Perform the play *Treemonisha* with or for a younger class or a group of senior citizens. (Lesson 15)
- Develop a school pride clean-up day, doing whatever work is necessary to improve the appearance of the school. (Lesson 8)
- Walk through a three-block area around the school. List things that could be done to improve the area such as cleaning up graffiti or picking up trash. Submit a report to the city council on the improvements. Select one of the improvements and do it. (Lesson 8)
- Create a "Helping Tree" board in your classroom where students who do some community or family service post a leaf on the tree throughout the year. At the end of every week, discuss the services students and adults perform in the community. (Lesson 8)
- Read to (or with) senior citizens or kindergartners. (Lesson 10)
- Create a book or make a quilt from the following activities and present the book or quilt to the relevant individuals or group. (Lesson 14)
  - ➤ Interview older adults about their traditions and ancestors. (Lesson 5)
  - ➤ Discuss favorite childhood books with senior citizens. (Any lesson)
  - ➤ Interview local senior citizens to create oral histories of immigrants and families whose ancestors immigrated to your state. (Lesson 5)
- Make gift bags filled with baked goods and books for children or adults or senior citizens in the hospital. The bags can be decorated with pictures of

characters from books you have been reading. The gift bags can be given to friends or family of students in the class. The books can be donated by the students' families. (Lesson 12)

- Create a "Welcome Book" that provides an overview of the school for students who are new to the school community. Students seek input from staff, families, and other members of the school community on content that would be most helpful. They illustrate the book with drawings, pictures, collages, and personal messages.

OUR SERVICE-LEARNING PLAN

We have decided to _____

for _____ .

These are the skills we will use in the project:

_____

_____

These are the other people we will ask to help us with the project:

_____

_____

This is the physical capital we will use:

_____

_____

These are other resources we will use:

_____

_____

These are intermediate goods we will use:

_____

_____

This is how we will acquire the resources and intermediate goods:

_____

_____

THE PLAN

This is the work that will be done, the people who will do it, and the dates by which the tasks will be finished.

Task	Who	When

APPENDIX TWO
Bibliography

Allard, Harry, and James Marshall. *Miss Nelson Is Missing.* New York: Houghton Mifflin Company, 1977. The children in Miss Nelson's class go beyond misbehaving; they are downright terrible! Near her wits' end, Miss Nelson thinks up a brilliant plan. The next day the kids have a substitute—the nasty Viola Swamp—who loads the boys and girls with homework and never gives them a story hour. By the time Miss Nelson finally returns, the children are so grateful they behave well. But now Viola Swamp is missing. **ISBN:** 0395252962

Atkin, S. Beth. *Voices from the Fields.* New York: Little Brown and Company, 1993. Photographs, poems, and interviews with nine children reveal the hardships and hopes of Mexican-American migrant farm workers and their families. **ISBN:** 0316056200

Averill, Esther. *The Fire Cat.* New York: Harper and Row, 1960. Pickles, the cat with the big paws, can't help being bad—he keeps chasing little cats up trees. When his friend Mrs. Goodkind gives him to Joe, the fireman, Pickles decides a firehouse cat is what he wants to be. He tries hard to help the firefighters at their jobs, but it isn't until Pickles proves he cares for the other cats that he earns his fire hat—and a seat on the fire truck. **ISBN:** 0064440389

Axelrod, Amy. *Pigs Go to Market.* New York: Simon & Schuster Books, 1997. Just in time for their big Halloween party, Mrs. Pig wins a free, five-minute shopping spree at the local supermarket. As she loads up her cart with goodies, young readers can polish their multiplication skills. The Pigs can't wait to throw their annual Halloween party. But when Grandpa and Grandma Pig eat all of the candy, the Pigs have to make a last-minute trip to the market. **ISBN:** 0689825536

Barasch, Marc Ian. *No Plain Pets!* New York: Harper Collins Publishers, 1994. A child enumerates the many exotic pets there are from which to choose, from a big black gorilla to an imaginary thing with six legs sticking out of its head. **ISBN:** 0064433757

Baylor, Byrd. *One Small Blue Bead.* New York: Atheneum Books, 1965. A boy makes it possible for an old man in their primitive tribe to go in search of other men in far-off places. **ISBN:** 0684193345

Baylor, Byrd. *Amigo.* New York: Aladdin paperbacks, 1992. Desperately wanting a pet to love, a boy decides to tame a prairie dog that has already decided to tame the boy for his own pet. **ISBN:** 0689712995

Baylor, Byrd. *The Desert Is Theirs.* New York: Aladdin Paperbacks, 1975. Simple illustrations describe the characteristics of the desert and its plant, animal, and human life. **ISBN:** 0689711050

Baylor, Byrd. *When Clay Sings.* New York: Aladdin paperbacks, 1972. The daily life and customs of prehistoric southwest Indian tribes are retraced from the designs on the remains of their pottery. **ISBN:** 0689711069

Berenstain, Stan, and Jan Berenstain. *The Berenstain Bears Get the Gimmies.* New York: Random House, 1983. Brother and Sister Bear want everything in sight, and they throw tantrums when they don't get what they want! Wisely, Mama and Papa deal with this universal childhood malady by teaching the cubs about the family budget and the importance of appreciating all they have already. **ISBN:** 0394805666

Berenstain, Stan, and Jan Berenstain. *The Berenstain Bears' Trouble With Money.* New York: Random House, 1983. To earn coins for the Astro Bear video game, Brother and Sister Bear find ways to work for money. They find the middle ground between being spendthrifts and little misers. **ISBN:** 0394859170

Berry, James. *Don't Leave an Elephant to Go and Chase a Bird.* New York: Simon & Schuster Books, 1995. Anancy Spiderman trades various items with the people he encounters, until he himself is distracted by a bird and ends up empty-handed. **ISBN:** 0689804644

Blood, Charles L. and Martin Link. *The Goat in the Rug.* New York: Aladdin Books, 1990. A goat named Geraldine, who lives on a Navajo reservation with Glenmae, a Navajo weaver, tells this story. One day, Glenmae decides to weave Geraldine into a rug. First Geraldine is clipped. Then her wool is spun into fine, strong yarn. Finally, Glenmae weaves the wool on her loom. **ISBN:** 0689714181

Blos, Joan W. *Old Henry.* New York: Marrow Williams and Company, 1990. When Old Henry sees a ramshackle house, he decides to move in, birds and all. His furniture seems to go with the place; he feels at home. But the neighbors expect Old Henry to fix up the house. They try everything to persuade him, but even the bribe of a hot pie won't get Old Henry to clean up. Tired of being nagged, he leaves town. Then the townspeople feel lost without him and, wherever it is that Old Henry is, he misses them, too. A letter to the mayor sets the wheels in motion for him to return home. **ISBN:** 0688099351

Bradby, Marie. *More Than Anything Else*. New York: Orchard Books, 1995. The nine-year-old narrator describes how he works with his father and brother in the salt works of West Virginia. The aches from his difficult labor are not as painful as the boy's longing to learn to read. When he sees a man reading a newspaper aloud, he knows that he, too, can learn. **ISBN:** 0531094642

Brott, Ardyth. *Jeremy's Decision*. New York: Kane/ Miller Book Publishers, 1990. This family oriented story has a strong message for girls, boys, and parents about expectations and achievements. Jeremy dreads being asked whether he will be a famous orchestra conductor like his father, and one day he musters the courage to announce his real ambition. **ISBN:** 0916291650

Brown, Marc. *Arthur's Pet Business*. Boston: Little, Brown & Company, 1990. Arthur's determination to prove he is responsible enough to have a puppy brings him a menagerie of animals to care for. **ISBN:** 0316113166

Bulla, Robert Clyde. *The Paint Brush Kid*. New York: Random House, 1999. Nine-year-old Gregory paints pictures representing the life of the Mexican-American old man known as Uncle Pancho and attempts to save him from losing his house. **ISBN:** 0679892826

Buller, Jon. *Pig at Work*. U.S.A: Troll Communications, 1998. This Level l Planet Reader follows Pig through his day at the Wolf Construction Company. **ISBN:** 0816743746

Bunting, Eve. *A Day's Work*. New York: Clarion Books, 1997. A touching immigration story about the reversal of roles between child and adult. A small Mexican-American boy, Francisco acts as interpreter for his *abuelo*, newly arrived in California and looking for work as a day laborer. The boy speaks English for his grandfather and pushes hard, even tells lies, to get him a job as a gardener. *Abuelo* is a carpenter, not a gardener, and he and Francisco pull out the flowers instead of the weeds. The employer is furious, but then *abuelo* takes charge and insists on working the next day without pay to put things right. In the tense competition among the laborers in the hiring yard, we feel the desperation of people without work. **ISBN:** 0395845181

Bunting, Eve. *Flower Garden*. Florida: Voyager Books Harcourt Inc., 1994. Helped by her father, a young girl prepares a flower garden as a birthday surprise for her mother. **ISBN:** 0152023720

Bunting, Eve. *Fly Away Home*. New York: Clarion Books, 1993. Andrew and his father are homeless; they live in an airport. In order to survive they must avoid notice, so they keep to themselves, changing terminals every night, sleeping sitting up. The yearning sadness of the story is ameliorated only by the obvious affection between father and son. **ISBN:** 0395664152

Bunting, Eve. *How Many Days to America*. New York: Clarion Books, 2000. After the police come, a family is forced to flee their Caribbean island and set sail for America in a small fishing boat. **ISBN:** 0899195210

Bunting, Eve. *Market Day*. USA: Harper Collins, 1996. Tess and Wee Boy observe the farm animals, wonder at the sword-swallower, hear the playing of pipes, and experience all the excitement of a country fair in Ireland. **ISBN:** 0060253649

Bunting, Eve. *Moonstick*. New York: Harper Collins Publishers, 2000. A young Dakota Indian boy describes the changes that come both in nature and in the life of his people with each new moon of the Sioux year. **ISBN:** 0064436195

Burton, Virginia Lee. *Mike Mulligan and His Steam Shovel*. Boston: Houghton Mifflin Company, 1977. Mike Mulligan proves that, although dated, his steam shovel is still useful. **ISBN:** 0395259398

Carlson, Nancy. *I Like Me!* New York: Penguin Group, 1988. An alphabet book that explores self-esteem. **ISBN:** 0140508198

Chinn, Karen. *Sam and the Lucky Money*. New York: Lee and Low Books Inc., 1997. This year Sam gets to spend his New Year's gift money any way he chooses. Shopping carefully in his favorite Chinatown stores, he is disappointed to find that everything he wants is too expensive. Deciding to forgo a tasty sweet or a new toy for himself, Sam donates his money instead to a barefoot homeless man. **ISBN:** 1880000539

Choi, Yangsook. *New Cat*. New York: Farrar Straus and Giroux, 1999. Shortly after coming to America, Mr. Kim, owner of a tofu factory in the Bronx, gets a fluffy silver cat that makes her home in his factory and one night saves it from burning down. **ISBN:** 0374355126

Deedy, Carmen Agra. *The Yellow Star*. Atlanta: Peach Tree Publishers LTD., 2000. Retells the story of King Christian X and the Danish resistance to the Nazis during World War II. **ISBN:** 1561452084

dePaola, Tomie. *The Art Lesson*. New York: Putnam & Grosset Groups, 1997. Tommy wants to be an artist when he grows up, and he can't wait to meet his art teacher when he gets to first grade. Then he finds out that she expects him to copy her pictures. Tommy knows real artists don't copy! But after some discussion, they find a solution that allows the artist in Tommy to shine. **ISBN:** 0698115724

dePaola, Tomie. *Helga's Dowry*. New York: Harcourt Brace Jovanovich, 1999. Helga, a troll, ventures into the world of people to earn her dowry to marry Lars, but things do not work out as she hopes. **ISBN:** 0833503618

dePaola, Tomie. *The Legend of the Indian Paintbrush*. New York: Putnam & Grosset Group, 1988. Little Gopher follows his destiny, as revealed in a dream vision, of becoming an artist for his people and eventually is able to bring the colors of the sunset down to earth. **ISBN:** 0698113608

dePaola, Tomie. *Oliver Button Is a Sissy*. New York: Harcourt Brace Jovanovich, 1979. Oliver Button didn't like to do the things that boys usually do. He didn't play ball very well, but he really liked to draw pictures and read and, most of all, dance. The boys teased him, and the girls stuck up for him, and on the school wall somebody wrote, "Oliver Button Is a Sissy!" But Oliver just practiced his dancing even harder. One day he'd show them all. **ISBN:** 0156681404

dePaola, Tomie. *Strega Nona*. New York: Aladdin Paperbacks, 1975. When Strega Nona leaves him alone with her magic pasta pot, Big Anthony is determined to show the townspeople how it works. **ISBN:** 0671666061

dePaola, Tomie. *Strega Nona Meets Her Match*. New York: Scholastic Inc., 1993. When Strega Amelia visits her "old friend," Strega Nona, she sees how well Strega Nona is doing with the old-fashioned ways, curing everything from lovesickness to hair loss. She's sure she can do better with her new-fangled equipment. Looks like Strega Nona has met her match, until Strega Amelia hires Big Anthony. A rival puts Strega Nona out of the healing business until Big Anthony's assistance inadvertently sabotages the newcomer in his usual well-meaning way. **ISBN:** 0698114116

Duggleby, John. *Story Painter*. San Francisco: Chronicle Books, 1998. A biography of the African American artist who grew up in the midst of the Harlem Renaissance and became one of the most renowned painters of the life of his people. **ISBN:** 0811820823

English, Karen. *Speak English for Us, Marisol!*. Morton Grove: Albert Whitman & Company, 2000. Marisol, who is bilingual, is sometimes overwhelmed when her Spanish-speaking family members and neighbors need her to translate for them. **ISBN:** 0807575542

Fiday, Beverly and David Fiday. *Time to Go*. Florida: Harcourt Brace Jovanovich, Publishers, 1990. As he and his family prepare to leave, a child takes one last look at their farm home. **ISBN:** 0152006087

Flanagan, Alice K. *A Busy Day at Mr. Kang's Grocery Store*. New York: Children's Press, 1997. Describes the work done each day by a Korean-American who owns the neighborhood grocery store. **ISBN:** 0516260618

Flanagan, Alice K. *A Day in Court with Mrs. Trinh*. New York: Children's Press, 1998. Explaining the work of a legal-aid attorney to a kindergarten audience is not an easy task. *A Day in Court* does a serviceable job; by necessity, the legal system is a bit oversimplified. **ISBN:** 0516262467

Flanagan, Alice K. *Learning Is Fun with Mrs. Perez*. New York: Children's Press, 1998. In Mrs. Perez's bilingual kindergarten class, learning is fun! This book introduces Mrs. Perez and her class and describes how she teaches each of her students in a special way. **ISBN:** 0516262955

Flanagan, Alice K. *Riding the School Bus with Mrs. Kramer*. New York: Children's Press, 1998. Text and photographs follow Mrs. Kramer, a safe and careful bus driver, and as she gets the children to school on time and brings them home again at the end of the day. **ISBN:** 0516264060

Fleischman, Paul. *Weslandia*. Cambridge: Candlewick Press, 1999. Wesley's garden produces a crop of huge, strange plants that provide him with clothing, shelter, food, and drinks, thus helping him create his own civilization and changing his life. **ISBN:** 0763600067

Flournoy, Valerie. *The Patchwork Quilt*. New York: Scholastic Inc., 1995. Tanya loves listening to her grandmother talk about the quilt she is making from pieces of colorful fabric from the family clothes. When Grandma becomes ill, Tanya decides to finish Grandma's masterpiece, with the help of her family. Using scraps cut from the family's old clothing, Tanya helps her grandmother and mother make a beautiful quilt that tells the story of her family's life. **ISBN:** 0803700970

Freeman, Don. *A Pocket for Corduroy*. New York: Puffin Books, 1978. A toy bear that wants a pocket for himself searches for one in a laundromat. **ISBN:** 0140503528

Galdone, Paul. *The Little Red Hen*. New York: Clarion Books, 1973. The little red hen finds none of her lazy friends willing to help her plant, harvest, or grind wheat into flour, but all are eager to eat the cake she makes from it. **ISBN:** 0899193498

Garza, Carmen Lomas. *Magic Windows*. California: Children's Book Press, 1999. In Spanish and English, Carmen Lomas Garza portrays her family's Mexican customs through cut-paper work. **ISBN:** 089239157

Garza, Carmen Lomas. *Making Magic Windows*. Boston: Allyn and Bacon, 1999. Author Carmen Lomas Garza is a pioneer in popularizing the traditional Mexican craft of papel picado in the United States and developing it into a sophisticated art form. This workbook shows children and their families how to create these beautiful papel picado designs and banners by simply folding and cutting tissue paper. **ISBN:** 0892391596

Gibala-Broxholm, Janice. *Let Me Do It!* New York: Bradbury Press, 1994. Four year-old Katie seeks to prove her independence to her family by trying to pour her milk, hold grandma's yarn, and perform other tasks all by herself. **ISBN:** 0027358275

Gilman, Phoebe. *Something from Nothing*. New York: Scholastic Inc., 1992. A modern adaptation of this favorite Jewish folktale describes how the blanket grandfather had made for young Joseph is transformed over the years into a jacket, a button, and, ultimately, a story. **ISBN:** 059047281X

Gurney, Nancy, and Eric. *The King, the Mice and the Cheese*. New York: Random House, 1965. A king's struggle to keep mice from devouring his favorite food makes an amusing circular tale. **ISBN:** 0394800397

Halperin, Wendy Anderson. *Once upon a Company*. New York: Orchard Books, 1998. At a loss for "something to do," Joel, Kale, and Lane take their mother's suggestion to make and sell Christmas wreaths. It could, she tells them, be the start for earning money for college. With the help of grandparents, classmates, friends, and local townspeople, the College Fund Wreath Company is born and becomes a success, even branching off into the Peanut Butter & Jelly Company during the summer seasons. **ISBN:** 0531300897

Hamilton, Virginia Shook. *Dry Longso*. New York: Harcourt Brace & Company, 1992. As a great wall of dust moves across their drought-stricken farm, a young man called Dry Longso, who literally blows into their lives with the storm, relieves a family's distress. **ISBN:** 0152242414

Hazen, Barbara. *Tight Times*. New York: Viking Press, 1979. A youngster isn't sure why a thing called "tight times" means not getting a dog. **ISBN:** 0140504427

Heilbroner, Joan. *Robert the Rose Horse*. Canada: Random House, 1962. Robert, a horse, has an allergy to roses; the allergy helps him catch some robbers. **ISBN:** 0394800257

Henkens, Kevin. *Lilly's Purple Plastic Purse*. New York: Greenwillow Books, 1996. Lilly loves everything about school: the pointy pencils, the squeaky chalk, the fish sticks and chocolate milk in the lunchroom, especially her cool teacher, Mr. Slinger. But when Lilly brings her purple plastic purse and its treasures to school and can't wait until sharing time, Mr. Slinger confiscates her prized possessions. Lilly's fury leads to revenge and then to remorse, and she sets out to make amends. **ISBN:** 0688128971

Herrera, Juan Felipe. *Calling the Doves (El Canto De Las Palomas)*. San Francisco: Children's Book Press, 1995. The author recalls his childhood in the mountains and valleys of California with his farm-worker parents who inspired him with poetry and song. **ISBN:** 0892391324

Herrera, Juan Felipe. *The Upside Down Boy*. California: Children's Book Press, 2000. *The Upside Down Boy* is Juan Felipe Herrera's memoir of the year his migrant family settled down so that he could go to school for the first time. Juanito is bewildered by the new school and misses the warmth of country life. Everything he does feels upside down: He eats lunch when it's recess, he goes out to play when it's time for lunch, and his tongue feels like a rock when he speaks English. But his sensitive teacher and loving family help him find his voice through poetry, art, and music. **ISBN:** 0892391626

Hoban, Lilian. *Arthur's Honey Bear*. New York: Harper & Row Publishers, 1974. Arthur decides to sell his old toys but is reluctant to part with his old bear. **ISBN:** 060223693

Hobbie, Holly. *Toot & Puddle*. Canada: Little Brown & Company, 1998. When he just about gives up trying to find the right birthday gift for Toot in Pip's Pet Shop, Puddle needs to look no further because the special present finds him. **ISBN:** 0316365564

Hoffman, Mary. *Amazing Grace*. New York: Dial Books, 1991. Grace loves stories, and with a boundless imagination she acts them all out. One day, her teacher asks who would like to play the lead in the play "Peter Pan." Grace eagerly raises her hand, but Raj tells her she isn't a boy, and Natalie tells her she can't because she is black. Nana sets Grace straight: she can do anything she sets her mind to! Grace's talent bursts forth, and she wins the audition hands down. **ISBN:** 0803710402

Holabird, Katharine. *Angelina and the Princess*. Wisconsin: Pleasant Company Publications, 1984. Angelina is too sick to dance well during the tryouts for the lead in the ballet; but when the leading ballerina sprains her foot, Angelina is ready to prove she is still the best dancer of all. **ISBN:** 1584851481

Hooks, William. *The Three Little Pigs and the Fox*. New York: Aladdin Paperbacks, 1989. Rooter, Oinky and their little sister, Hamlet, are three little pigs who aren't so little. They're getting bigger and bigger, and Mama decides it's time they each get homes of their own. She advises them to build strong houses, visit her each Sunday, and to watch out for that tricky old fox. When her brothers appear to be missing, can Hamlet outfox the fox? **ISBN:** 068980962X

Hopkinson, Deborah. *Sweet Clara and the Freedom Quilt*. New York: Alfred A. Knopf, 1995. As a seamstress in the Big House, Clara is luckier than the slaves who work in the fields. Still, she dreams of a reunion with her Momma, who lives on another plantation—and even of running away to freedom. When she hears two slaves wishing for a map to the Underground Railroad, she realizes how she can make a "freedom quilt" map that no master will ever suspect. **ISBN:** 0679874720

Hutchins, Pat. *The Doorbell Rang*. New York: Mulberry Books, 1989. Ma makes some freshly baked cookies, and her two kids sit down to eat them when ding dong! the doorbell rings! More kids arrive to share the cookies, but just when they sit down, ding dong! Finally, when there is only one cookie for each child, the doorbell rings again. Who is it? Grandma with a new tray of fresh baked cookies! And no one bakes cookies as good as Grandma's! Hutchins sneaks a bit of math into this funny tale. **ISBN:** 0688092349

Isadora, Rachel. *At The Crossroads*. New York: HarperCollins Children's Books, Greenwillow Books, 1994. A simple story about a group of black South African children awaiting the homecoming of their fathers, who have been working in distant mines for several months. **ISBN:** 0688131034

Jimenez, Francisco. *La Mariposa*. Boston: Houghton Mifflin Company, 1998. Because he can speak only Spanish, Francisco, son of a migrant worker, has trouble when he begins first grade, but his fascination with the caterpillar in the classroom helps him begin to fit in. **ISBN:** 0618073175

Johnston, Tony. *Slither McCreep and His Brother Joe*. San Diego: Harcourt Brace & Company, 1992. In a twisting tale of sibling rivalry, Slither McCreep develops a scheme to get back at his brother, Joe, for being a stingy reptile. **ISBN:** 0152761004

Joosse, Barbara. *The Morning Chair*. New York : Clarion Books, 1995. Bram and his parents leave their small town in Holland to settle in New York City. Missing the familiar sights, sounds, and tastes of home, and trying to adjust to the different way of life that confronts all newcomers, Bram still manages to keep his spirits up. Although he refuses to like green olives, and searches in vain for a glimpse of the promised mountains and cowboys, he finds comfort in the familiarity of possessions from home. Especially important is the morning chair in which he and his mother share cups of tea with milk, Dutch cookies, and quiet time. **ISBN:** 0395623375

Julius, Lester. *From Slave Ship to Freedom Road*. New York: Dial Books, 1998. Portrays the story of slavery from its beginnings on the famous ship of the Middle Passage to centuries of subjugation for the enslaved Africans and, finally, hard-won freedom for their descendants. This gifted artist has vividly expressed both the horror of the slaves' experience and the hope and spirit of resistance that sustained the survivors. **ISBN:** 0803718934

Kasza, Keiko. *The Wolf's Chicken Stew*. New York: G.P. Putnam's Sons, 1987. In an effort to fatten up Mrs. Chicken for his delicious stew, Wolf unwittingly makes some new friends. The wolf is an endearing critter whose expressions run the gamut from sly to shy to downright lovable. **ISBN:** 0698113748

Kimmel, Eric A. *Four Dollars and Fifty Cents*. New York: Holiday House, 1989. To avoid paying the Widow Macrae the four dollars and fifty cents he owes her, deadbeat cowboy Shorty plays dead and almost gets buried alive. **ISBN:** 0823410242

Kirk, Daniel. *Trash Trucks*. New York: Putnam, 1997. Are they beasts, or great machines that feast to keep our city clean? Very imaginative artwork and text tell the story of trash trucks with eyes, mouths, and hands devouring piles and piles of garbage. The rhyming text follows two kids as they race around town following the trash truck. Three of the trucks save the kids when a pile of trash almost falls on them. **ISBN:** 0399229272

Klinting, Lars. *Bruno the Baker*. New York: Henry Holt and Company, 1997. Bruno, the lovable birthday beaver, is baking a birthday treat with his little buddy, Felix. The simple engaging text and the easy-to-follow recipe at the end of the book will encourage future bakers. **ISBN:** 0805055061

Kraus, Robert. *Big Squeak, Little Squeak*. New York: Orchard Books, 1996. Two mice are tired of eating cheese curls, and go to the neighborhood cheese store. It's run, unfortunately, by a Mr. Kit Kat, who seems very nice, but once mice enter his store they never come out! But Little Squeak manages to get the best of Mr. Kit Kat, who will never bother mice again. **ISBN:** 053109474X

Kraus, Robert. *Leo the Late Bloomer*. New York: Windmill Books, 1994. Leo, a young tiger, finally blooms under the anxious eyes of his parents. **ISBN:** 006443348X

Kroll, Virginia. *Pink Paper Swans*. Michigan: Eerdmans, 1994. Eight-year-old Janetta Jackson is fascinated by the skill with which Mrs. Tsujimoto folds (origami) boxes, birds, whales, cats, and crabs to sell to local gift shops. The book concludes with directions for making a simple swan, with standard diagrams. **ISBN:** 0802850812

Lamarche, Jim. *The Raft*. New York: Harper Collins Publishers, 2000. Nicky isn't one bit happy about spending the summer with his grandma in the Wisconsin woods, but then the raft appears and changes everything. As Nicky explores, the raft works a subtle magic, opening up the wonders all around him—the animals of river and woods, his grandmother's humor and wisdom, and his own special talent as an artist. **ISBN:** 0688139787

Lasker, Joe. *Mothers Can Do Anything*. Canada: George J. McLeod, 1977. Text and illustrations demonstrate many occupations of mothers including plumber, dentist, subway conductor, and others. **ISBN:** 0807552879

Lawrence, Jacob. *The Great Migration*. New York: Harper Collins Publishers, 1995. A series of paintings chronicles the journey of African Americans who, like the artist's family, left the rural South in the early twentieth century to find a better life in the industrial North. **ISBN:** 0060230371

Leaf, Munro. *The Story of Ferdinand*. New York: Puffin Books, 1977. All the other bulls would run and jump and butt their heads together. But Ferdinand would rather sit and smell the flowers. So what will happen when our pacifist hero is picked for the bullfights in Madrid? Originally published over 50 years ago, this story of the bull who preferred smelling flowers to fighting has become a favorite for generations of children. **ISBN:** 0140502343

Lester, Helen. *Tacky the Penguin*. Boston: Houghton Mifflin Co., 1988. Tacky the penguin epitomizes tackiness. He dresses in Hawaiian shirts, greets friends with a slap on the back, and sings dreadfully! All the other penguins are put off by Tacky's behavior, but when some rough hunters come by, Tacky's manners send them packing too! Tacky may be odd, but he sure is a good penguin to have around! **ISBN:** 0395562333

Lewin, Ted. *Amazon Boy*. New York: Macmillan Publishing Company, 1999. The author of *When the Rivers Go Home* returns to Brazil for a look at the mouth of the Amazon, as seen by a boy whose father takes him on a birthday excursion from their jungle home to coastal Belem. Paulo and his father travel downriver on a small steamer, see fishermen selling their catch in the city's harbor, and admire a huge filhote, a species endangered by over-fishing. After wandering the market, they set out for home, the father commenting sadly on the thoughtless degradation of forest and river. Lewin rounds out his simple story with Paulo catching a valuable filhote and letting it go. **ISBN:** 0027573834

Lewin, Ted. *Market*. New York: Lothrop Lee & Shepard Books, 2000. We are transported to various markets throughout the world to discover some of the wonders to be found there. The text and pictures tell a captivating and convincing story of local culture. **ISBN:** 0688121616

Lin, Grace. *The Ugly Vegetables*. Watertown: Charlesbridge, 1999. A little girl can't help but wonder why she and her mom are growing plants in their garden that are so different from the pretty flowers their neighbors have. Mom says they are growing something better than flowers, but the little girl is not convinced until they harvest the vegetables they have grown, and something unexpected happens. **ISBN:** 0881063363

Lipson, Greta B., and Baxter Morrison. *Fact, Fantasy and Folklore*. Carthage: Good Apple Inc., 1977. Through role playing and insightful questions, teachers can help students investigate the "rights" and "wrongs" of fairy tales such as Rumplestiltskin, Jack of Beanstalk fame, the Mayor of Hamlin who didn't pay the piper, and many more. **ISBN:** 0916456110

Lorbiecki, Marybeth. *Sister Anne's Hands*. New York: Penguin Group, 1998. It's the early 1960s, and Anna has never seen a person with dark skin—until she meets Sister Anne. At first she is afraid of her new teacher, but she quickly discovers how wonderful Sister Anne is. Then one of Anna's classmates directs a racist remark toward Sister Anne. The teacher's wise way of turning the incident into a powerful learning experience has a profound impact on Anna. **ISBN:** 0140565345

Lowell, Susan. *The Tortoise and the Jackrabbit*. Arizona: Northland Pub., 1994. Tortoise is an aged granny decked out in flower-brimmed hat, lace-trimmed anklets, and white gloves. Hare sports a bandanna and a feather in his hat along with his cocky, sure-to-win attitude. The spectators represent many other native desert critters humorously dressed in western attire. As the competitors advance on the course, indigenous plants and lesser-known animals are inconspicuously identified. While Tortoise slowly, appreciatively, and deservedly munches her championship bouquet of spring flowers, the author seizes the opportunity to apply this well-known tale to contemporary concerns about the destruction of desert habitat. If the wild desert is preserved, Lowell concludes, "we will all be winners." **ISBN:** 0873585860

Lucado, Max. *Just the Way You Are*. Wheaton: Crossway Books, 1999. When a compassionate king decides to adopt three orphaned children, the townspeople begin to offer advice: "You need to impress the king." But, as this story shows, not all kings want to be impressed. **ISBN:** 1581341148

Lund, Jillian. *Way Out West Lives a Coyote Named Frank*. New York: Dutton Children's Books, 1992. Whether he's hanging out with his friends, chasing rabbits, mixing it up with a Gila monster, or pondering the setting sun, Frank is one smooth character. **ISBN:** 014056232X

Madrigal, Antonio Hernandez. *Erandi's Braids*. New York: G. P. Putnam's Sons, 1999. In a poor Mexican village, Erandi surprises her mother by offering to sell her long, beautiful hair in order to raise enough money to buy a new fishing net. **ISBN:** 0399232125

Maestro, Betsy. *The Story of Money*. New York: Houghton Mifflin Company, 1993. A history of money, from the barter system in prehistoric times, to the first use of coins and paper money, to the development of the modern monetary system. **ISBN:** 0688133045

Manuel, Lynn. *Fifty-five Grandmas and a Llama*. Layton: Peregrine Smith Book, 1997. Sam wishes constantly for a grandma. His search proves futile until he places a classified ad in the newspaper. Talk about results! Fifty-five grandmas, one with a llama, appear in no time, and he decides to keep them all. However, their hovering and hugging soon overwhelm him. He places another ad, this one for boys and girls needing grandmas. Soon the ladies depart with new children to love. Only the one with the llama remains. **ISBN:** 0879057858

Martin Jr., Bill. *Knots on a Counting Rope*. New York: H. Holt, 1997. A young Native American boy begs his grandfather to tell him about the day he was born and other events in his young life. The poetic language touches the reader, as does the story of this blind boy and his courage in overcoming that form of darkness in his life. What could be sad is instead upbeat and inspirational, as is the love and respect between the boy and his grandfather. **ISBN:** 0805054790

Martin, John. *Once Upon a Dime*. New York: Federal Reserve Bank, 1993. *Once Upon a Dime* is an excellent, interesting, and exciting program for teaching young students about money.

Martinez, Alejandro Cruz. *The Woman Who Outshone the Sun*. San Francisco: Children's Book Press, 1991. Retells the Zapotec legend of Lucia Zenteno, a beautiful woman with magical powers who was exiled from a mountain village and takes its water away in punishment. **ISBN:** 089239126X

Mayer, Mercer. *Just for You*. New York: Golden Press, 1975. Young readers see Little Critter trying very hard to be a good helper. Unfortunately, something always seems to get in his way. When he tries to dry dishes for his mother, the dishes grow slippery. When he makes an effort not to splash water out of the tub, a storm comes up. On and on it goes, with Little Critter and his good intentions making readers laugh with him from start to finish. **ISBN:** 030711838X

Mayer, Mercer. *Just Me and My Dad*. New York: Golden Press, 1977. It's the tale of a father-and-son camping trip filled with Little Critter's mistakes and good intentions. In spite of difficulties, however, the happy father and son manage to put up their tent, catch fish for dinner, and sleep beneath the stars. **ISBN:** 0307118398

Mayer, Mercer. *Gator Cleans House*. New York: Random House Incorporated, 1995. Gator's friends come over to help clean house and end up making an even bigger mess. **ISBN:** 0679873546

McCullough, L. E. *Plays of People at Work*. Lyme: Smith and Kraus, 1998. "What do I want to do when I grow up?" These 12 original plays follow a quartet of bright, inquisitive grade-schoolers as they visit friends and family at real-life work sites. The introduction to each play includes details about the nature of the work, educational and training requirements. **ISBN:** 157525140X

McMullan, Kate. *Fluffy and the Firefighters*. New York: Scholastic Inc., 1999. After firefighters visit Ms. Day's classroom, Fluffy gets a chance to see what they do first hand. **ISBN:** 0439129176

McMullan, Kate. *Fluffy Goes to School*. New York: Scholastic Inc., 1997. Fluffy the guinea pig suffers many humiliations at the hands of the students in Ms. Day's classroom. **ISBN:** 0590372130

McPhail, David. *Drawing Lessons*. Boston: Little, Brown and Co., 2000. A bear explains how he became an artist, first experimenting with simple drawings, then continuing to draw things around him and things in his imagination. Includes tips for drawing. **ISBN:** 0316563455

McPhail, David. *Those Can-Do Pigs*. New York: Dutton Children's Books, 1996. Come meet the Can-Do Pigs as they do just about anything and everything you can imagine, from flying to the moon to baking cakes, from tickling generals to charming snakes. **ISBN:** 0140562567

Medearis, Angela Shelf. *Picking Peas for a Penny*. New York: Scholastic Inc., 1990. Angeline and John are off on a pea-picking race. Grandfather has promised them a penny for every pound of peas they pick on a hot summer day during the Depression. But what can the children buy for just a few pennies? Lots of things. This rollicking, rhyming text provides an upbeat, historical portrait of an African-American farm family. **ISBN:** 0938349546

Medearis, Angela Shelf. *Treemonisha*. New York: H. Holt, 1995. Treemonisha, the daughter of freed slaves in the post-Civil War South, gets an education and devotes herself to lifting her people out of poverty and ignorance. **ISBN:** 0805017488

Merriam, Eve. *Daddies at Work*. New York: Aladdin Picture Books, 1996. A good focus on the family and fathers. Ethnic diversity. **ISBN:** 0689809980.

Merriam, Eve. *Mommies at Work*. New York: Aladdin Picture Books, 1989. Examines many different jobs performed by working mothers, including counting money in banks and building bridges. **ISBN:** 0689809999

Miller, Margaret. *Who Uses It?* New York: Mulberry Books, 1990. A hammer. A rolling pin. A water can. A paintbrush. Guess who uses these and other tools of the trade? Adults at work and children at play. **ISBN:** 0688170579

Miller, William. *The Bus Ride*. New York: Lee and Low Books, Inc., 1998. A black child protests an unjust law in this story loosely based on Rosa Parks' historic decision not to give up her seat to a white passenger on a bus in Montgomery, Alabama, in 1955. **ISBN:** 1880000601

Miller, William. *Richard Wright and the Library Card*. New York: Lee & Low Books, 1999. A seventeen-year-old African-American borrows a white man's library card and devours every book as a ticket to freedom. As a boy in the segregated South, young Richard Wright was determined to borrow books from the public library. **ISBN:** 1880000881

Mills, Lauren A. *The Rag Coat*. Boston: Little Brown & Company, 1991. With paintings that capture the beauty of Appalachia in authentic detail, this tender story about a resourceful mountain girl's special coat will touch readers with its affirming message of love and friendship. **ISBN:** 0316574074

Miranda, Anne. *To Market, to Market*. San Diego: Harcourt Brace & Company, 1997. Starting with the nursery rhyme about buying a fat pig at market, this tale goes on to describe a series of unruly animals that run amok, evading capture and preventing the narrator from cooking lunch. **ISBN:** 0152000356

Mitchell, Margaree King. *Uncle Jed's Barbershop*. New York: Simon and Schuster Books, 1997. In the segregated South of the 1920s, Uncle Jed was the only black barber in a county of sharecroppers. He always dreamed of owning his own barbershop, but his generous heart and some bad luck during the Depression forced him to defer that dream for years. Finally, on his 79th birthday, Uncle Jed opened the doors of his new shop. **ISBN:** 0689819137

Mora, Pat. *Tomas and the Library Lady*. New York: Alfred A. Knopf, 2000. Mora tells the fictionalized story of one summer in his childhood during which a librarian in Iowa, who takes him under her wing while his family works the harvest, fosters his love of books and reading. She introduces him to stories about dinosaurs, horses, and American Indians and allows him to take books home where he shares them with his parents, grandfather, and brother. When it is time for the family to return to Texas, she gives Tomas the greatest gift of all—a book of his own to keep. **ISBN:** 0375803491

Moss, Marissa. *Mel's Diner*. Mahwah: Bridgewater Books, 1996. Mabel has lots of fun helping her parents in the diner. She talks to customers, listens to their stories, sets the table, cleans the counter, and dances to the jukebox music with her friend Rhoda. **ISBN:** 0816734615

Moss, Marissa. *Rachel's Journal*. Florida: Harcourt Brace & Company, 1998. In her journal, Rachel chronicles her family's adventures traveling by covered wagon on the Oregon Trail in 1850. **ISBN:** 0152018069

Neitzel, Shirley. *The House I'll Build for the Wrens*. New York: Greenwillow Books, 1997. Cumulative verses describe all the tools that a young boy borrows from his mother's toolbox to make a bird house. **ISBN:** 068814731

Numeroff, Laura Joffe. *If You Give a Moose a Muffin*. New York: HarperCollins, 1991. If a big hungry moose comes to visit, you might give him a muffin to make him feel at home. If you give him a muffin, he'll want some jam to go with it. When he's eaten all your muffins, he'll want to go to the store to get some more muffin mix. **ISBN:** 0060244054

Numeroff, Laura Joffe. *If You Give a Mouse a Cookie*. New York: Harper & Row, 1985. If a hungry little traveler shows up at your house, you might want to give him a cookie. If you give him a cookie, he's going to ask for a glass of milk. He'll want to look in a mirror to make sure he doesn't have a milk mustache, and then he'll ask for a pair of scissors to give himself a trim. The consequences of giving a cookie to this energetic mouse run the young host ragged. **ISBN:** 0060245867

Numeroff, Laura. *If You Give a Pig a Pancake*. New York: Harper Collins Juvenile Book, 1998. If you give a pig a pancake, she'll want syrup to go with it. You'll give her some of your favorite maple syrup, she'll probably get all sticky, so she'll want to take a bath. She'll ask you for some bubbles. One thing leads to another when you give a pig a pancake. **ISBN:** 0060266864

Paulsen, Gary. *The Tortilla Factory*. San Diego: Harcourt Brace, 1998. The text traces the journey of corn from harvest and grinding to the tortilla factory. By concentrating on hands rather than on the individual faces of the workers, the oil-on-linen paintings demonstrate respect for the ethic of hard work and hold broad, universal appeal. **ISBN:** 0152016988

Paulsen, Gary. *Worksong.* San Diego: Harcourt Brace & Company, 1997. A lyrical depiction of the world of labor expresses the work ethic with sensitivity and dignity and celebrates the quiet grace of everyday life, explaining how each worker contributes to the larger human process. **ISBN:** 0152009809

Peet, Bill. *Jethro and Joel Were a Troll.* Boston: Houghton Mifflin, 1990. The good half of a two-headed troll gets them both in trouble when he lets the bad side rule for a day. The unpredictable outcome rounds out the fun and embodies a kernel of good sense, showing the advantages when wiser heads prevail. **ISBN:** 0395539684

Peet, Bill. *Kermit the Hermit.* Boston: Houghton Mifflin Company, 1965. After a mean, selfish crab is rescued by a little boy, the crab searches for a way to repay the kindness. **ISBN:** 0395150841

Phipps, Barbara, Martha C. Hopkins, and Rita L. Littrell. *Teaching Strategies K-2.* New York: National Council on Economic Education, 1995. **ISBN:** 156183470X

Polacco, Patricia. *Chicken Sunday.* New York: The Putman & Grosset Group, 1992. The hatred sometimes engendered by racial and religious differences is overpowered by the love of people who recognize their common humanity. After being initiated into a neighbor's family in a solemn backyard ceremony, a young Russian-American girl and her African-American "brothers" determine to buy their "gramma" Eula a beautiful Easter hat. But their good intentions are misunderstood, until they discover just the right way to pay for the hat. **ISBN:** 0698116151

Polacco, Patricia. *The Keeping Quilt.* New York: Simon & Schuster Books for Young Readers, 1998. "We will make a quilt to help us always remember home," Anna's mother said. "It will be like having the family back home in Russia dance around us at night." And so it was. From a basket of old clothes, Anna's babushka, Uncle Vladimir's shirt, Aunt Havalah's nightdress, and an apron of Aunt Natasha's become The Keeping Quilt, passed along from mother to daughter for almost a century. For four generations the quilt is a Sabbath tablecloth, a wedding canopy, and a blanket that welcomes babies warmly into the world. **ISBN:** 0689820909

Polacco, Patricia. *Thank You Mr. Falker.* New York: Philomel Books, 1998. Little Trisha is overjoyed at the thought of starting school and learning how to read. But when she looks at a book, all the letters and numbers just get jumbled up. Her classmates make matters worse by calling her dummy. Only Mr. Falker, a stylish, fun-loving new teacher, recognizes Trisha's incredible artistic ability—

and her problem—and takes the time to lead her finally and happily to the magic of reading. **ISBN:** 0399231668

Polacco, Patricia. *The Trees of the Dancing Goats*. New York: Scholastic Inc, 1996. During a scarlet fever epidemic one winter in Michigan, a Jewish family helps make Christmas special for their sick neighbors by making their own Hanukkah miracle. **ISBN:** 0689808623

Polacco, Patricia. *My Ol' Man*. New York: Scholastic Inc., 1995. Patricia and Ritchie spend the summer in Michigan with their father and paternal grandmother. Their parents are divorced. Their dad is a traveling salesman who tells them incredible stories about his journeys—like the story of the magic rock he finds one day on his way home. The stories become serious when Dad loses his job, and it's not until somebody outside the family recognizes the magic in his tales that things turn right again. **ISBN:** 0590897500

Priceman, Marjorie. *How to Make an Apple Pie and See the World*. New York: Dragonfly Books, 1994. An apple pie is easy to make. . .if the market is open. But if the market is closed, the world becomes your grocery store. First hop a steamboat to Italy for the finest semolina wheat. Then hitch a ride to England and hijack a cow for the freshest possible milk. And, oh yes! Don't forget to go apple picking in Vermont! A simple recipe for apple pie is included. **ISBN:** 0679880836

Prigger, Mary Skillings. *Aunt Minnie McGranahan*. New York: Clarion Books, 1999. When Aunt Minnie McGranahan inherits nine orphaned nephews and nieces, the neighbors think it will never work. Aunt Minnie is small and tidy, and she lives alone in a neat little house. She has a neat little garden and a neat little barn, and she has a system for everything. Certainly there's no place in her life for children. But Aunt Minnie is a problem solver, and she surprises everyone by bringing home all nine children and coming up with clever new systems to accommodate her expanded family. It turns out Aunt Minnie likes children after all! **ISBN:** 039582270X

Rathmann, Peggy. *Officer Buckle and Gloria*. New York: G. P. Putnam's Sons, 1995. The children at Napville Elementary School always ignore Officer Buckle's safety tips, until a police dog named Gloria accompanies him when he gives his safety speeches. **ISBN:** 0399226168

Ray, Mary Lyn. *Pumpkins*. San Diego: Harcourt Brace Jovanovich, Publishers, 1992. Emblems of autumn, pumpkins are portrayed in many guises. **ISBN:** 015201358X

Rockwell, Anne. *Career Day*. Harper Collins Publisher, 2000. On Career Day the children in Mrs. Madoff's class take turns introducing special visitors. Every visitor has something interesting to share, and together the class learns about the work different people do. **ISBN:** 0060275650

Rockwell, Anne. *Only Passing Through*. New York: Alfred A. Knopf, 2000. Isabella was only nine when she was sold for the first time. And at first no one wanted her. The slave auctioneer had to throw in a flock of sheep before someone bid on the skinny young girl. But this young girl would grow. She would grow to become a brave, strong, towering woman who would speak out against the evils of slavery. She would transform herself into one of the most powerful voices of the abolitionist movement and would help to change the course of a nation. **ISBN:** 0679891862

Ryan, Pamela Munoz. *Doug Counts Down*. New York: Disney Press, 1998. Count down with Doug as he tries unsuccessfully to persuade customers that Peanutty Buddies aren't so delicious after all. **ISBN:** 0786831413

Rylant, Cynthia. *A Little Shopping*. New York: Simon & Schuster, 2000. Three cousins spend a year living with their Aunt Lucy while their parents tour Europe with a ballet company. The girls get along beautifully, think of wonderful projects, and adore their aunt and her charming boyfriend. **ISBN:** 0689817096

San Souci, Robert D. *The Snow Wife*. New York: Dial Books for Young Readers, 1993. When a Japanese woodcutter breaks his promise and describes his encounter with a terrifying snow woman, he loses his wife and must take a dangerous journey to win her back. **ISBN:** 0803714092

Say, Allen. *Grandfather's Journey*. Boston: Houghton Mifflin, 1993. This autobiographical reminiscence describes the wanderlust of the author's grandfather, who is torn between love for his native Japan and for California. Missing one place while in the other, the grandfather is always longing to be where he isn't. The grandson inherits his grandfather's love of travel, and, like him, longs to be in both places at the same time. **ISBN:** 0395570352

Schroeder, Alan. *Carolina Shout!* New York: Dial Books, 1995. A young girl describes the music she hears in the cries of various vendors on the streets of Charleston, South Carolina. **ISBN:** 0803716761

Schwartz, M. David. *If You Made a Million*. New York: Lothrop, Lee & Shepard Books, 1989. Describes the various forms which money can take, including coins, paper money, and personal checks, and how it can be used to make purchases, pay off loans, or build interest in the bank. **ISBN:** 0688070183

Seuss, Dr. *Oh, The Places You'll Go*. New York: Random House, Inc., 1990. Seuss' familiar pajama-clad hero is up to the challenge, and his odyssey is captured vividly in busy two-page spreads evoking both the good times (grinning purple elephants, floating golden castles) and the bad (deep blue wells of confusion). Seuss' message is simple but never sappy: life may be a 'Great Balancing Act,' but through it all "There's fun to be done." **ISBN:** 0679805273

Silverman, Erica. *Big Pumpkin*. New York: Macmillan Publishing Company., 1992. A witch is assisted by a ghost, vampire, mummy, and bat when pulling her pumpkin off the vine. Then they all feast cheerfully on pumpkin pie. **ISBN:** 0689801297

Simon, Carly. *Amy the Dancing Bear*. New York: Doubleday, 1989. Amy dances tirelessly until the moon is high despite her mother's efforts to get her to bed. Ultimately, it is Amy who tucks Mother in and finally readies herself for sleep. **ISBN:** 0385266375

Soto, Gary. *Chato's Kitchen*. Canada: The Putnam & Grosset Group, 1995. To get the "ratoncitos," little mice who have moved into the barrio, to come to his house, Chato the cat prepares all kinds of good food: fajitas, frijoles, salsa, enchiladas, and more. **ISBN:** 0698116003

Spinelli, Jerry. *Maniac Magee*. New York: Scholastic, 1991. After his parents die, Jeffrey Lionel Magee's life becomes legendary as he accomplishes athletic feats and other extraordinary exploits that awe his contemporaries. **ISBN:** 0316809063

Spurr, Elizabeth. *Mama's Birthday Surprise*. New York: Hyperion Books, 1996. Pepe and his brother and sister love the stories about their legendary, faraway Uncle Cesar. True, the stories do seem to change a bit each time Mama tells them. But Mama has always reassured them that if they are ever in trouble, wealthy Uncle Cesar will instantly come to their rescue with "a bushel basket of pesos." When the kids concoct a plan to reunite Mama with her long-lost uncle, their mysterious family hero turns out to be the biggest (and best) surprise of all. **ISBN:** 0786811242

Stanley, Diane. *Woe Is Moe*. New York: G.P. Putman's Sons, 1995. Moe, from Moe the Dog in Tropical Paradise, works beside his best friend, Arlene, at the Frozen Cow Ice Cream Factory. Every Friday night they share dinner at the Happy-All Chinese restaurant. Then Moe is promoted to vice president. He may be in the fast lane now, but Moe's also sad and lonely—until a message in a fortune cookie sends him back to Arlene. **ISBN:** 0399226990

Stevens, Janet, and Susan Crummel Stevens. *Cook-A-Doodle-Doo!* New York: Harcourt Brace & Company, 1990. With the questionable help of his friends, Big Brown Rooster manages to bake strawberry shortcake, which would have pleased his great-grandmother, Little Red Hen. **ISBN:** 0152019243

Stevens, Janet. *The Three Billy Goats Gruff*. San Diego: Harcourt Brace & Company, 1987. Three goats live on a stony mountain, while across the valley they can see a lovely green grass meadow. But the only way to get there is by the old bridge. And under the bridge lives a horrible troll, who gobbles up anyone who tries to cross. **ISBN:** 0152863974

Stevens, Janet. *Tops & Bottoms*. San Diego: Harcourt Brace & Company, 1995. Hoping to rise above his level of poverty, clever Hare strikes a deal with a rich and lazy bear in which Bear will contribute the land while Hare will provide the labor for a profitable harvest. **ISBN:** 0152928510

Stewart, Sarah. *The Money Tree*. Canada: Harper Collins, 1991. In summer many people harvest the leaves on the strange tree growing in Miss McGillicuddy's yard, but when Miss McGillicuddy thinks about needing firewood for the winter, she realizes the tree may have another use. **ISBN:** 0374452954

Surat, Michele. *Angel Child, Dragon Child*. New York: Scholastic Inc, 1989. Ut has just come to the United States from Vietnam, and she does not like her new American school. The children all laugh when she speaks in Vietnamese. And there's that awful red-haired boy named Raymond, who picks on her almost every day. Most of all, Ut misses her mother who had to stay behind in Vietnam. But to Ut's surprise, it is Raymond who thinks of the perfect way to help her. **ISBN:** 0606041567

Tolstoy, Leo. *Philipok*. New York: Philomel Books, 2000. Philipok's mother had told him that he is too young to go to school, but one day he sets out to go on his own. **ISBN:** 0399234829

Torres, Leyla. *Saturday Sancocho*. New York: A Sunburst Book/ Farrar, Straus & Giroux, 1995. Bright cheerful illustrations capturing the spirit of the marketplace and a recipe for delicious chicken sancocho highlight the tale of Maria Lili and her grandparents and the special Saturday when they run out of everything but eggs. **ISBN:** 0374464510

Tso, Donald, and Sylvia Tso. *Dream Catchers*. New York: Troll Communications L.L.C, 2000. The Tsos recreate the Native American tradition of making dream catchers—hoops hung by the Ojibwe Indians on their children's cradleboards to "catch" bad dreams. **ISBN:** 0816736030

Viorst, Judith. *Alexander, Who's Not (Do You Hear Me? I Mean It!) Going to Move*. New York: Aladdin Paperbacks, 1995. Angry Alexander refuses to move away if it means having to leave his favorite friends and special places. **ISBN:** 0689820895

Viorst, Judith. *Alexander, Who Used to Be Rich Last Sunday*. New York: Aladdin Paperbacks, 1978. Although Alexander and his money are quickly parted, he comes to realize all the things that can be done with a dollar. **ISBN:** 0689711999

Waters, Kate, and Madeline Slovenz-Low. *Lion Dancer*. New York: Scholastic Inc., 1990. Describes six-year-old Ernie Wong's preparations for the Chinese New Year celebrations and his first public performance of the lion dance in New York's Chinatown. **ISBN:** 0590430475

Weidt, Maryann N. *Mr. Blue Jeans*. Minneapolis: Carolrhoda Books, Inc., 1992. This is a biography of the immigrant Jewish peddler who went on to found Levi Strauss & Co., the world's first and largest manufacturer of denim pants. Carefully selected details brighten an account of the industrious immigrant who became a highly successful and respected San Francisco businessman. **ISBN:** 0876145888

Wells, Rosemary. *Fritz and the Mess Fairy*. New York: Dial Books, 1991. Fritz drives his family crazy because he is so messy about everything he does. When his mother asks him to do the dishes one evening, he suddenly realizes his science project is due. The project is unsuccessful, and Fritz goes to bed leaving a big mess everywhere. While he sleeps, a fairy appears from the science project. She wakes up Fritz and begins making an even bigger mess all over the house. Fritz finally realizes that being messy is not a good way to live and vows to live a neater life. **ISBN:** 0803709811

White, Linda. *Too Many Pumpkins*. New York: Holiday House, 1998. Pumpkins—stewed, baked, steamed, mashed, boiled, roasted, and rotten. No more pumpkins! And so it was that Rebecca Estelle never allowed a pumpkin into her home until. . . the day an enormous pumpkin falls off a truck and smashes into her yard. In a few months those "slimy pumpkin smithereens sprout up into a sea of pumpkins." Her solution of what to do with them is sure to bring on the giggles. **ISBN:** 0823413209

Whiteley, Opal. *Only Opal*. New York: Philomel Books, 1994. Born around 1900, young Opal was only five years old when she began to keep her diary. She had barely learned how to print, but was already expressing her thoughts. This is the story of one year in Opal's life with her adopted family, frequently uprooted as they move from one lumber camp to another. **ISBN:** 0399219900

Whitford-Paul, Ann. *Eight Hands Round*. New York: HarperCollins, 1996. In early American times, almost every house had a patchwork quilt, sewn together from hundreds of pieces of fabric. Each quilt was unique, with different combinations of fabrics and colors and a distinct pattern. But who developed these patterns? And what did they mean? Whitford-Paul's fascinating text describes 26 different quilt patterns, placing each in its historical context. From the Anvil, used to shape horseshoes and farm tools, to the Zigzag, which symbolized the lightning that streaked across the open sky, this is a creative look at a meaningful folk art tradition. Complemented by Jeanette Winter's bold art, this patchwork alphabet is the perfect way to learn about an important period in American history. **ISBN:** 0064434648

Williams, Sherley Anne. *Working Cotton*. San Diego: Harcourt Brace Jovanovich, 1997. Shelan is the third of four daughters in a family of African-American migrant workers. She narrates one day in their lives as they work in the fields picking cotton. Although she is too young to do much, the girl helps pile cotton for her mother, who carries baby Leanne as she works. Sometimes, she befriends other children. Finally, the sun sets, the bus comes, and the tired laborers take their bundles and leave. **ISBN:** 0152014829

Williams, Vera B. *A Chair For My Mother*. New York: William Morrow & Co., 1982. A child, her waitress mother, and her grandmother save dimes to buy a comfortable armchair after all their furniture is lost in a fire. **ISBN:** 0688040748

Wing, Natasha. *Jalapeño Bagels*. New York: Simon & Schuster, 1996. Pablo can't decide what to take to school for International Day. He wants to pick something from the bakery his parents own, something that represents his heritage, but what? There are the pan dulce and chango bars his Mexican mother prepares, but the bagels and challah made by his Jewish father are equally tempting. Then, when Pablo begins to help his parents prepare the Sunday morning baking, he comes up with the perfect choice. **ISBN:** 0689805306

Wolf, Bernard. *Beneath the Stone*. New York: Orchard Books, 1994. The customs and daily life of a small village in Oaxaca, Mexico, are shown through the eyes of six-year-old Zapotec Indian boy. **ISBN:** 0531068358

Wood, Audrey. *Jubal's Wish*. New York: The Blue Sky Press, 2000. It's a beautiful, sunny day, and Jubal Bullfrog has prepared a delicious picnic lunch to share with his friends. Skipping down the flower path, he's so happy his feet barely touch the ground. But Gerdy Toad is much too busy and much too grumpy to share Jubal's picnic lunch. And Captain Dalbert Lizard is tired and depressed. How Jubal wishes he could do something to make his friends as happy as he is on this glorious day. When Jubal plops down beneath a daisy and closes his eyes, something magical and unexpected happens. Jubal is granted a wish. Is this a dream? But Jubal's wish does comes true, in a warm and memorable way. **ISBN:** 043916964X

Zemach, Margot. *The Little Red Hen*. New York: Farrar, Straus and Giroux, 1983. A retelling of the traditional tale about the little red hen whose lazy friends are unwilling to help her plant, harvest, or grind the wheat into flour, but all are willing to help her eat the bread that she makes from it. **ISBN:** 0374445117

Zimelman, Nathan. *How the Second Grade Got $8,205.50 to Visit the Statue of Liberty*. Illinois: Albert Whitman & Company, 1992. Chronicles the triumphs and setbacks of the second grade as the students try a variety of schemes to raise money for a trip to the Statue of Liberty. **ISBN:** 0807534315

APPENDIX THREE
Glossary

Advantage: A desirable (good) consequence of an alternative.

Alternative: A possible choice; one of two or more possible actions or choices; opportunities from which people choose.

Benefit: Something that satisfies or helps to satisfy a want.

Capital resource: A product, such as machine, tool, or building used to produce other goods or services; can also refer to physical capital.

Choice: A selection from two or more alternatives.

Consequence: Something that happens as a result of an action or event.

Consumer: A person whose wants are satisfied by using goods or services; a person who buys and uses goods or services.

Cost: What one gives up when deciding to do something; for instance, a decision referring to production or a payment for productive resources.

Creativity: The use of imagination to make something new or different.

Criteria: Guidelines for making decisions; the values given to qualities of alternatives when a choice is made.

Decision making: The process of selecting a choice.

Disadvantage: An undesirable (bad) outcome of an alternative.

Economics: The study of decision making.

Entrepreneur: A person who organizes other productive resources, takes risks, and finds new ways of combining resources to produce a product.

Entrepreneurship: The ability and willingness to take risks and combine resources in a new way to produce a better product.

Goal: Something that a person wants to have or do.

Good: An object that can be used to satisfy a person's wants.

Human capital: The quality of labor resources which can be improved through investments in education, training, and health; skills and knowledge. (See also labor resources.)

Human resources: The quantity and quality of human effort directed toward producing goods and services. (See also labor resources or human capital.)

Improve: To make better.

Incentive: A reward or penalty that affects a person's well-being or ability to satisfy wants.

Income: Wages or salary payments for human capital; payments for productive resources (rents, wages, interest, or profit).

Innovation: The introduction of an invention into a use that has economic value.

Innovator: A person who introduces an invention into a use that has economic value. (See also entrepreneur.)

Input: Resource or intermediate good.

Interdependence: Two or more persons or groups depending on each other.

Intermediate goods: Products that are used up in the production of goods and services.

Interview: A meeting in which one person asks specific questions of another person to gather specific information.

Invention: A new product.

Investment in human capital: Development of skills and knowledge.

Knowledge: Awareness and understanding of facts and relationships.

Labor market: An interaction of people who want to work and people who want to hire workers.

Land resources: Gifts of nature; resources that are present without human intervention. (See also natural resources.)

Lesson plan: A plan that is developed ahead of time that provides the steps to teach something.

Market: An interaction of buyers and sellers.

Natural resources: Gifts of nature; resources that are present without human intervention. (See also land resources.)

Obstacle: Something that gets in the way of reaching a goal.

Opportunity cost: The value of the best-known alternative given up when a choice is made.

Output: A product (good or service).

Physical capital: Goods produced and used to produce other goods and services. (See also capital resources.)

Practice: To do something many times for the purpose of learning.

Produce: To use inputs and a plan to make goods and services.

Producer: One who uses productive resources to make goods and services.

Product market: An exchange of goods and services by producers and consumers.

Production: Using resources to produce a good or service.

Production plan: A method for producing a good or service.

Productive resource: Natural resources (land), human resources (labor, human capital), capital goods (physical capital) or entrepreneurial resources available to produce goods and services. (See also factors of production.)

Productivity: Usually output per worker.

Re-evaluate: To think again about a decision made previously.

Resources: Things that can be used to produce goods or services.

Resource market: An exchange of productive resources.

Responsibility: Accepting the consequences of choices.

Scarcity: The condition of not being able to have all of the goods and services one wants.

Service: An action that can satisfy a person's wants.

Service learning: Learning by doing something for someone else; providing a service.

Skill: Something that a person can do.

Specialization: When people concentrate their production on fewer goods and services than they consume. Specialization increases productivity, but also requires trade and increases interdependence.

Technology: New tools, machines, or methods used for production; application of new tools, machine or processes to solve a problem.

Trade-off: Choosing between the expected value of one opportunity against the expected value of its best alternative.

Wage: The price of labor or human resources (salary).

Wants: Desires that can be satisfied by consuming a good, service, or leisure activity (economic wants).

Work: Human physical or mental effort used in production of goods or services.

Worker: A person who does work.